GOLF CLASSICS

General Editor

LAWRENCE VINEY

Other titles available:

BETTER GOLF

BETTER GOLF

BY

PERCY ALLISS

WANNSEE GOLF AND COUNTRY CLUB, BERLIN
FORMERLY OF WANSTEAD GOLF CLUB

WITH AN INTRODUCTION BY
GEORGE W. GREENWOOD
AND SIXTEEN ACTION
PHOTOGRAPHS BY HORACE GRANT

A & C BLACK · LONDON

First published in 1926 by
A & C Black, Ltd, London

Published in paperback in 1990 by
A & C Black (Publishers) Ltd,
35 Bedford Row, London WC1R 4JH

ISBN 0 7136 3309 3

A CIP catalogue record for this book is
available from the British Library

Printed in Great Britain by BPCC Wheatons Ltd, Exeter

CONTENTS

CONTENTS

LIST OF ILLUSTRATIONS

(between pages 22 and 23)

INTRODUCTION

NOT without a certain amount of justification Percy Alliss has been described as " the Vardon of the younger school of golfers." To say this means that the swing is true and correctly applied to the main business—that of hitting the ball. The cultivation of the true rhythmical swing, where there is an entire absence of jerkiness and forcing, is three-fourths of the battle. Without the true swing no lasting progress can be made in golf, and nothing but disappointment pursues the footsteps of the player.

In his admirable book, *Better Golf*, Alliss shows how this true swing can be attained, and a careful study of the principles enunciated will be well repaid. He puts forward no new and startling ideas because he is firmly convinced that golf is best played and learned in the simplest manner possible, and that all attempts at theorising should be strictly avoided. The book is notable for its sound golf sense and also for the absence of puzzling calculations and anatomical treatises. There is nothing in the twenty chapters that the ordinary mortal cannot understand, and by the exercise of average intelligence cannot assimilate.

This is not a book dedicated solely to the beginner; there is material in it which will not only intrigue the player with a single-figure handicap, but which is calculated materially to help him on the road to greater success and achievements in this most enthralling game. Alliss is well qualified to broadcast a message to golfers, for he has twice been Champion of Wales and Essex respectively, and the greater prizes cannot elude him much longer.

I would wish to stress the point that I have had nothing whatever to do with the writing or the compilation of the book.

GEORGE W. GREENWOOD.

March, 1926.

BETTER GOLF

CHAPTER I

CHOICE AND CARE OF CLUBS

THE number of golf clubs a beginner needs
is six : Driver, Spoon, No. II Iron, Mashie,
Niblick and Putter. These will keep him
well occupied for a year or more, and with
them he can play any shot in the game.
Additional clubs are bought to supplement
these six, making the game easier by enabling
the player always to make a full shot instead
of the difficult half-stroke.

Thus the Mashie Niblick is taken for a lie
that calls only for a half-shot with the Mashie,
and is yet too much for the Niblick. The
Jigger finds its place between the Mashie and
the No. II Iron, while for longer play than a
No. II Iron there comes the No. I Iron before
the Spoon. For work that the Spoon cannot
manage, but which is insufficient for the

Driver, there is the Brassie. These four extra clubs divide up the range of distances for which each of the six is suited and consequently leave much less to human judgment. So that a full set consists of ten clubs, all of which will be appreciated at their proper value when the essential six have been entirely mastered.

A golfer demands at least two things of his clubs : that they should suit him as an individual, and that they should wear well. There are players, of course, who ask much more than this, and expect the tools to supply the deficiencies of the workman. It is no easy matter to find six clubs that are not only serviceable but also well fitted to their prospective user. Undoubtedly the most satisfactory plan for the beginner is to buy his clubs from the professional who is to give him lessons. In this way he will not only get expert judgment as to the clubs best suited to his height and build, but will also arouse the interest of the pro. and so add considerably to the value of his lessons. A man who has given his life to the study of the game, who is constantly teaching golf and handling a great variety of clubs, must obviously gain knowledge that makes him eminently qualified to give advice in the selection of a good set. If he is to teach a beginner in the game he is naturally anxious that his pupil should be properly equipped and able to do justice to his lessons.

Even a professional has his limitations. He can pick out, for example, two or three drivers that are of suitable weight and length, but the final choice must be with the purchaser. Presuming that he has never before handled a golf club, he may fairly ask what is to guide him in a selection of one in several that are so much alike. Instinct alone can help him to choose.

Extremes in clubs are to be avoided, particularly in regard to weight and length. The great majority of players are happiest with a weight between 12 and 13 ounces, and anything above 13½ I should class as an extreme. Those who have tried reasonably hard and long, and yet have failed to acquire the vital snap with the wrists on hitting the ball, may find it possible to increase the speed of their club-head by using a heavy club. There cannot, of course, be the same life and length in a shot which is so bolstered up as there is in the result of crisp wrist action, nevertheless the heavy club is a measure that the desperate can fall back upon as a last resort.

I have found from experience that the average player is much best suited with a shaft of medium length.   Just as some hope to improve their game with the assistance of a heavy weapon, so others literally labour under the impression that a long shaft will give added power to their strokes.   They base their belief on a law of elementary mechanics by which it is accepted that the longer the handle of the hammer the harder the blow. But the swing in golf is a more involved and delicate motion than the wielding of a hammer.   A long club puts so great a strain on the wrists that they cannot perform their proper functions in making the   stroke. Further, it is not possible to put the whole weight of the body behind a shot with too long a club.   Especial care should be taken in this respect when selecting iron clubs, since they call for greater deftness in wielding than do the wooden clubs

There is a certain balance and suppleness of shaft that gives to a club that quality best defined as " feel." The club-maker who is possessed of real craftsmanship spends a great deal of time in testing and adjusting in pursuit of this quality, and it is too much to expect that products of factory piece-work will have received sufficient attention to endow them with the supremely important attribute of satisfactory " feel." No two clubs are exactly the same, but it is the ambition of every reputable player to replace his proved but worn-out friends by others as nearly like them as possible. Weight, materials, measurements may all be identical but the elusive something may still be wanting to make the similarity in any way real. The perfect wooden club, as I conceive it, should have a head of medium size and a carefully tapered shaft, not too thick under the grip and with the slightest bit of give near the head ; its weight would be between $12\frac{1}{2}$ and 13 ounces. Some golfers hold that the shaft should be absolutely stiff and unyielding, others believe that springiness and a certain amount of life are desirable. I would not

contradict the upholders of either opinion,
for they merely advocate for general use that
which they have proved best suited to
themselves.

It is a fortunate individual who knows what
suits him.   Often a pupil has handed me a
club that was a favourite when new, but has
apparently lost all its virtue.   Invariably the
particular club was totally unsuited to its
owner :   he imagined that it was made
especially for his style and in the first flush
of blind confidence no doubt used it creditably,
but disillusionment rapidly brought with it a
proper measure of the club's capabilities.

Two important considerations in making
a choice of clubs are the amount of loft that
each possesses, and the lie, which is governed
by the angle between shaft and head.   Here,
again, the safest course lies in an avoidance
of extremes.   The consequences of using a
club-face that is too much lofted are as
undesirable as those caused by too straight
a face.   It is advisable to discover with the
help of a pro. the degree of loft best adapted
to the individual style, and then to make
certain that the set of clubs is graded accord-

ingly. Far too often I have seen in the same bag a straight-faced Mashie and a lofted Iron, and similar misfits.

The grading of loft in a set should be a matter of considerable care : from the No. I Iron down to the Niblick it should increase in proportionate degrees. Thus the difference between the Mashie and the Jigger should be the same as that between the Jigger and the No. II Iron. It is, of course, ridiculous to have the two Irons with faces equally straight or nearly so, yet every pro. knows of such cases. Quite a number of players possess a full set only by name, two clubs out of the bag being so nearly alike that for all practical purposes they are the same. It is worth while examining one's clubs to see whether they are lofted in the proper order and to the proper extent ; immediate benefit will result from corrections in this respect.

The lie of the club-head decides how near to the ball a player must take his stance : when the sole of the club is placed squarely on the ground behind the ball, the shaft slants up to the hand at an angle governed by that at which it is joined to the head. Perhaps the

most important point in this respect concerns
the Driver and the Brassie. These should
have exactly the same lie, for they are wielded
in a similar manner; the extent of the
uprightness or otherwise of the shaft is again
a matter for the individual, but there is no
argument whatever for varying this between
the two clubs.

Personally, I prefer for the Spoon a rather
more upright lie. This naturally brings me
nearer the ball, and I find I am the more
easily able to pick it up from a close and
difficult position. Both of my Irons have a
medium lie, while the Jigger, Mashie and
Mashie Niblick are a little more upright;
in this way I obtain a more comfortable
position, standing up to the ball, and the sole
of the club is still on the ground from heel
to toe.

Like anything else subjected to such strain,
a golf club will wear out. Particularly is this
the case with a Driver: the head will
deteriorate and the shaft will become played
out and dead. It is always best to have two
Drivers, as nearly alike as it is possible to
get them, and to use them alternately for

several weeks at a time. I very seldom play more than two months at a stretch with the same Driver, and the clubs derive noticeable benefit from their rest. The iron club is stiffer in the shaft and does not need the same safeguarding from over-work.

There are more obvious ways of preserving the clubs in good condition, known to most golfers, but not practised by so many. Such, for instance, is the careful handling of the bag : time and again I see it dropped with a clatter that is the death-rattle of the wooden clubs as the iron heads take pieces out of their necks. A chipped and dented shaft cannot be so true and efficient as the perfect club.

One of the virtues of golf as a game is that it can be played in wet weather. A wet club should always be thoroughly dried, and the shaft will be the better for a drop of oil. To the real golfer who respects his clubs as much as he does the game this may seem unnecessary advice. To him I freely apologise for mentioning such matters.

Just as the cricketer cares for his bat and the billiard-player his cue, so too should the golfer take a pride in the condition of his clubs.   At least once a month they should be oiled and polished ; only if treated in this way can they be fairly expected to give efficient and lasting service.   The knowledge that the clubs are the best for his style and in perfect condition will give their owner invaluable confidence. Finally, remember that a sportsman never neglects his gun, however bad the day's shooting.

CHAPTER II

VERY few golfers appreciate fully the importance of correct grip. The way in which the club is held by the hands may at first seem a small concern beside the more obvious essentials of stance and swing. Nevertheless, any shot can be made or marred by the grip, and I find some defect in this direction in ninety per cent. of the beginners and players who come to me for advice.

There are two very definite reasons why the club should be held in one particular way. The first reason is that of ensuring exact impact with the ball on as many occasions as possible. Experience has shown that there is one grip better than the rest, by which a player has most certainty of bringing the club-head back to the ball exactly as he addressed it. A man whose eye is good may hold the club as he pleases and still succeed in hitting the ball quite frequently, but to hit

it at the right spot with consistent accuracy
and with the face of the club at the right angle
he must adopt a grip which in some measure
conforms with that most generally accepted.

The second reason affects wristwork. In
other and less pleasant sciences than golf it
is commonly understood that the combined
effect of two units is invariably greater than
that which results when they are used
separately. So that two wrists worked in
harmonious conjunction are a great deal
better than the same two wrists exerting their
strength independently. To get the maximum amount of power from the wrists the
club must be wielded in such a way that the
utmost co-operation is allowed. Only in this
way will a player do full justice to his
strength in playing the ball.

A bad grip means that one if not both of
these desirable effects is lost, either the ball
will be struck at the wrong angle or the blow
will be feeble in proportion to the amount of
energy expended.

Before describing the mechanism of the
grip it may be well to say at once that some
of the greatest exponents of the game differ

in their methods of holding the club. The difference, however, lies only in comparatively insignificant detail. Alex Herd, Mitchell and Vardon all use different grips, but in each case the root principles are the same. It is merely in the position of their fingers that the distinction lies, for all three hold their wrists in the same position. Vardon prefers to grip with his fingers, Herd with the palm and fingers, while Mitchell's method lies between the two. Always the club is so held that full benefit is derived from the wrists.

Perseverance in the use of a proper grip is, perhaps, one of the most irksome rules in the discipline of golf. The natural way of holding the club is the wrong way, and the force of instinct is soon realised by every beginner. At first it is always easier to hit the ball further and with greater accuracy by relying merely on the eye and caring nothing for an orthodox grip. But no progress towards proficiency can be made unless patience is taken to master what seems at first to be an extraordinarily awkward and uncomfortable hold. In the same way a violinist will at

first revolt against the discomfort that falls
to the lot of his left wrist; it is apparently
clumsily placed, it aches, there are many
other ways of holding the violin, but not
otherwise can such effects be produced. A
golfer has to withstand the temptation to
quarrel with what appears to him to be an
entirely wrong principle. Once the correct
grip has been mastered there will be an ample
harvest of the fruits of patience.

There is no more eloquent explanation of
the grip than that supplied by photographs.
A study of Plates II and III should in itself
be sufficient instruction, but it will not be
out of place to draw attention to certain
points that must not be overlooked. The
left hand is the more important in gripping
the club, since it is the left wrist that com-
mands the club during the swing. It will be
seen later that such variations of the straight
drive as pulling and slicing are primarily the
concern of the left wrist.

An actual description of the grip should be
as concise and clear as possible, but in any
case it must be very carefully followed if any
good is to result. The sole of the club having

been laid on the ground in its natural position, the shaft falls diagonally across the fingers of the upturned left hand from the top joint of the forefinger to the root of the little finger. As the fingers close on the shaft the thumb is brought over to touch the tip of the forefinger. The wrist is now pressed gently downwards and slightly to the right into a position immediately above the shaft. In Plate II it will be seen that the back of the left hand and the knuckles of the first and second fingers are turned well to the front and upwards.

With the shaft running diagonally across the fingers as before, the right hand is now brought into position below the left. The little finger of the right hand is placed on the knuckle of the left forefinger, and the three remaining fingers of the right hand grip the club close up against the left. As in the case of the left hand, the right thumb touches the tip of the forefinger. The top of the left thumb is now completely covered by the ball of the right. Finally, the right wrist is pressed gently to the left and the grip is tightened and complete.

If this grip is properly made it will be
found to give control and length in playing
any straight shot. There are some who
favour a change of grip, as, for instance, in
the case of driving and putting, but in my
own experience any attempt at change is the
reverse of beneficial. Far better to master
one method of holding the club and to employ
it always.

Circumstances occasionally demand that
the ball should be pulled or sliced. Since the
correct grip is one of the greatest assets in
obtaining straightness it follows that some
change of grip must be made if the flight of
the ball is to deviate from a direct line. To
slice, the whole grip is moved round a little
to the left, so that the back of the left hand
faces towards the hole. The right hand is
brought well over the left, its back and
knuckles facing upwards.

For the pull the grip is taken more than
ordinarily on the right of the shaft. The
back of the left hand should be very square
to the front and facing the sky, while the right
hand goes almost underneath the shaft with
the knuckles turned towards the ground.

This procedure is in fact a reversal of that followed in making a slice.

For the sake of the emphasis that it deserves, I would repeat that if a correct grip can be made instinctive by patience and perseverance it cannot fail to be of the greatest advantage in every part of the game.

CHAPTER III

It has often been said that the player who drives a long ball has little or no advantage over the short driver. If the long driver cannot control his ball, this contention is justified. But well-controlled length in driving is about half the battle in golf.

One of the finest exponents of driving that England has ever had is Abe Mitchell. His accuracy and length place him high above the several well-known players who can drive a longer ball. Although a regular entrant for the long-driving competition, held at the championship each year, Mitchell has never won it. There is an undeniable pleasure in hitting a really long drive, and it is perfectly justified ; but as soon as accuracy of direction is sacrificed to distance, then one of the most delightful strokes in golf becomes merely a feat of strength. A comparatively short drive down the middle of the fairway gives more real joy than a tremendous flier that is lost in the distance and in the rough. And, what is still more important, it is infinitely better golf.

Nevertheless, I should not for one moment suggest that the aspirant to perfection should for ever deny himself the satisfaction of full-blooded hitting and remain a martyr to un-impeachable straightness. A balance must be held between the two factors of length and accuracy, and the beginner especially must remember that it is easier to develop length after having mastered direction than it is to tame wild hitting into a reasonable sub-jection.

Three fundamentals form the broad basis of this much-desired combination of length and accuracy : a good stance, free and perfect pivoting from the hips, and a strong and supple wrist. It is of little use to keep the eye fixed earnestly on the ball if the feet are incorrectly placed, body-stiffness will cancel the advantage of the most expensive and beautiful of clubs, while all the practice in the world will not make a satisfactory drive unless the wrists and forearms have a certain

wiry suppleness to give a telling whip at the
bottom of the swing.

First, and perhaps most important of all,
the stance. For the straightforward drive
the stance should be a study in symmetry,
there should be equal distribution of weight
and consequently perfect balance. Beginners
frequently ask how far apart they must place
their feet, as though golf were an exact
exercise in measurement and quantities, a
mere matter of mathematics. The width
between the feet depends entirely upon the
individual, and chiefly upon length of leg.
In many cases it will be found that a comfortable stance will be obtained if the heels are
roughly the same distance apart as the width
of the shoulders. A player must judge for
himself the distance of his straddle ; he must,
as it were, wedge his weight firmly and
comfortably within the span of his legs.

A distinct " bite " on the ground with the
inside of the feet and a balanced comfortable
feeling are signs that the space between the
toes is approximately correct. Plate IV,
illustrating my stance, shows the weight
borne equally by the feet, with the head

Plate I.   FINISH OF THE DRIVE.

Plate II.   STANCE FOR THE DRIVE.

The feet are slightly open and the weight equally distributed. Both arms straight,
but not stiff, and the right shoulder brought forward. The shaft of the club at right
angles to the line of flight.

Plate III.　　　　THE DRIVE.　TOP OF SWING.

Both wrists are beneath the shaft, which is barely horizontal.　While the body has
pivoted round to the right the head has not moved.

Plate IV.   THE SPOON. STANCE.

The right foot is almost at right angles to the line of flight, the left turned well out.   Otherwise the stance is the same as that adopted for the drive.

Plate V. THE SPOON. TOP OF SWING.

The pivot of the shoulders is full, but the left foot still takes its share of weight on the inside of the toe.   The extreme point of the club-head is pointed directly downwards.

Plate VI.   THE SPOON. FINISH OF SWING.

Perfect balance has been kept in the transition to an exactly opposite position to
that at the top of the swing. The club is carried well over the left shoulder.

Plate VII.   THE NO. I IRON.   ADDRESS.

Head, hands and club-head are in one straight line.   The right shoulder is in a
good striking position, and both arms are straight.   The stance is slightly open
but the shaft remains exactly at right angles to the line of flight.

Plate VIII.   THE NO. I IRON. TOP OF SWING.

The left shoulder is above the centre of a line joining the toes.   The left arm is extended, and the toe of the club points to the ground.

Plate IX.   THE NO. I IRON.   FINISH OF SWING.

The maintenance of balance is well shown.   Note should be taken of the position of right toe and knee.

Plate X.   THE NO. II IRON. STANCE.

The stance is an open one, the left toe being turned outwards and the ball
nearer the left heel than the right.

Plate XI.   THE NO. II IRON.   TOP OF SWING.

The full extent of the back swing with this club should never be greater than
shown above.   Both wrists are clearly seen directly under the shaft.

Plate XII.   THE NO. II IRON. FINISH.

A full follow-through, with the club-head carried well behind. The left foot
has fallen back exactly into its first position.

Plate XIII   THE MASHIE.   STANCE.

The photographs of Mashie play may be applied to the playing of short shots
generally.   Both arms are held well in to the body, and the club-face is slightly
open.   The ball is equidistant from both heels.

Plate XIV.   THE MASHIE NIBLICK. STANCE.

Both stance and club face are plainly open. The shoulders are turned in the
direction of the hole, right knee and arm being bent more than left.

Plate XV.   THE MASHIE NIBLICK.   TOP OF SWING.

The straight left arm and full pivot of the shoulders are noticeable.   The club-
head points up to the sky ; its position should be compared with that in Plate
XII.   The raising of the left heel is here a matter of choice.

Plate XVI.   THE STANCE FOR PUTTING.

Right foot, club-head and shaft are all exactly at right angles to the line of play.
The ball is opposite the left heel.   Both knees are bent and the body held in a
relaxed, half-sitting position, with the elbows turned slightly outwards

immediately above the centre of a line between them. Such photographs should be studied carefully and in considerable detail, for to the intelligent they can tell far more than innumerable pages of letterpress. Particular notice should be taken of the angle at which the toes point in relation to the ball, their position being a consideration of much importance in the matter of balance. It will be seen, too, that the left foot is an inch or two behind the right; in other words, it is a slightly open stance.

It should never be forgotten that when the club-head lies behind the ball preparatory to driving, the shaft must be at right angles to a direct line from the tee to the hole which is the objective. This is perhaps obvious, but it is one of those commonplaces that mean so much and yet are so often overlooked.

There remains the vexed question of how advice should be given concerning the distance from the ball at which a driver should take his stand. One will counsel a club-length between the ball and the bent knee; another will talk of " soling " the club perfectly level on the ground—a procedure that leaves room for an unfortunately wide margin of error; yet a third will mystify and confound the mind with a wide variety of diagrams, calculations and photographs obscured by dotted lines.

To my mind the simplest method of judging this distance is to stand beside the ball as if about to drive it with the club in the right hand alone. The right arm is straight and the shoulder brought well into a striking position; at the same time the poise of the body must be strictly maintained.

The necessity of standing square and erect on the tee cannot be over-emphasised. If shoulders are allowed to droop forward during the swing, the all-important feature of balance will suffer and disastrous consequences ensue. The whole weight of the body must be taken directly by the legs, there must be no overhanging of the upper parts to be supported. Here again, invaluable help will be found in a close study of the photograph.

If any one particular part of the body can be said to be of more importance than the rest in making preparations to drive, it is the knee. However freely one may pivot from the hips, the whole perfection of balance and swing will be destroyed if the knees are braced too stiffly or held too loosely. It is not an uncommon sight to see a player addressing the ball with his legs straight and knees stiff. Few worse mistakes are possible. As in other instances, comfort is the chief criterion : the knees must sag just sufficiently to give ease of position and to avoid the fatal tensing of nerves and muscles.

Having achieved his stance, the player next proceeds to reap the reward of patience by the actual effort of driving. Since the object is to hit the ball truly at the bottom of the swing, the first movements leading up to this contact must be examined. In purely mechanical terms, the ball is driven by swinging the club against it. This swing, however, must be so controlled that it brings the face of the club against one particular spot on the ball with consistent and meticulous accuracy. For purposes of analysis and instruction it is convenient to deal with the swing in three parts, but it must be borne in mind throughout that the swing in golf is not a series of separate movements, but a smooth and rhythmic whole. The first phase is the back-swing or lifting of the club to strike. The shoulders are moved round to the right, the left shoulder and knee coming in towards the ball, the right shoulder being turned to the rear. At the same time the club-head is taken back close to the ground and brought over the right shoulder. The greater part of the work in this preliminary swing is done by the left arm, which must be kept extended and straight, and by the wrists, which lever the club upwards over the right shoulder.

At the top of the swing both wrists should be beneath the shaft, the right elbow should point towards the ground and the left arm lie across the chest. The wrists must not bend *too* much at this point and the shaft of the club should barely reach the horizontal; the position is well illustrated by Plate VI.

The commencement of the downward swing is the work of the wrists. They force the club-head back into the same curve by which it ascended, and co-operate in swinging it down through the same arc against the back of the ball. The shoulders are turned round again to the front and the right arm and shoulder arrive in line just behind the ball, the arm and the club being in one perfectly straight line and the shoulder in the same position as when the ball was addressed. At the same time the wrists are whipped or snapped, as it were, through the ball. The harmonious working of these movements must, of course, become instinctive by practice. It would be impossible to remember consciously each essential and put the whole into action with sufficient rapidity to drive the ball from the tee.

The third phase of the drive is the follow-through after the actual hitting of the ball. This is a natural continuation of the downward swing which is in no way broken by contact with the ball. The salient point of the follow-through is the desirability of carrying, or rather throwing, the head of the club after the ball. The head and eyes remain facing the spot which the ball has left, while the club-head follows out along its line of flight as far as possible, and the right shoulder goes round under the chin. Both arms should be kept straight until the completion of the swing over the left shoulder.

During the downward swing the left heel regains its original position firmly on the ground, and in the follow-through the right heel is allowed to rise.

Much attention should be paid to correct footwork. In such games as cricket and tennis, in which a moving ball is the objective, the greatest contribution to proficiency is made by such footwork as places the player in the most advantageous position for making his stroke. The same principle applies in golf, but there is less excuse for imperfection because the ball is stationary.

In order to acquire this chief foundation of really good golf the beginner would be well advised to watch the balance of first-class professionals or amateurs. He will see how well the balance of the weight in maintained throughout the swing. On the backward swing the centre of gravity falls exactly between the feet. As the club makes its downward swing and strikes the ball the weight of the body is transferred slightly, but only slightly, on to the inside of the left foot, which receives the balancing assistance of the right toe.

Among my pupils I find that one of the most common faults is that of slicing. It is just as easy to slice when a straight drive is required as it is difficult to effect a slice for a specific purpose. In nine cases out of ten the trouble lies in too upright a swing. When

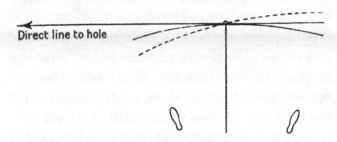

THE SLICED DRIVE.

The dotted line shows the incorrect swing which is the cause of slicing ; the unbroken line represents the correct arc described by the club head in relation to the desired line of flight. Feet placed for successful drive.

swinging too much over the ball it is not possible to hit it on that essential point which is furthest from the hole. The ball is swept off at a tangent by a swing of the club-head, which moves round it instead of straight through towards the hole. If the consistent slicer will cut his stroke short early in the follow-through he will see that his club-head is travelling by no means along the direct line from tee to hole, but has curled away to the left. Nor, for that matter, is the ball on its intended journey straight from tee to green.

The cause of too upright a swing lies partly in bad pivoting and partly in lifting the club-head from the ground too soon. The shoulders should pivot or turn a fraction of a second before the club is moved from behind the ball to the backward swing. This will give the desired sweeping of the club-head back across the surface of the grass before it actually rises; if it is lifted too soon, a swing that is too upright cannot fail to result. The preliminary sweep along the ground ensures a swing of the proper angle.

An incorrigible slicer will often be noticed hurrying his swing back, and he invariably improves his play on being told to take things more easily and slowly. At the same time I would warn the reader that the old maxim of " Slow back " can very easily be overdone. Too slow an action is stiff and disjointed, and it makes the timing of the swing a matter of infinite difficulty.

Long handicap men frequently neglect what is known as the " waggle " of the club when taking their stance, and there are writers on golf who condemn it as a fetish. But my own opinion is that its importance is far greater than is apparent. A player may be seen before he makes his swing standing absolutely still, then when he actually starts his swing there is an ugly jerk that at once ruins any grace and rhythm his movements may otherwise possess. The reason is obvious. He has, during the preliminary pause, stiffened up every muscle and tensed every nerve until all semblance of freedom has entirely disappeared. The best players always waggle in settling down to drive, and I have found that here again it pays to imitate them. None of them are still in addressing the ball, but club and wrists are kept moving smoothly and steadily until the final grounding of the club-head before the backward swing. During the waggle the shoulders should not be allowed to move more than is necessary to give perfectly free movement to the arms. Besides ensuring freedom of movement, the waggle is an invaluable means of measuring

distance from the ball and obtaining a good
striking position.

Of common faults in driving, over-swinging
is probably the mistake most often seen. By
this I mean the carrying back of the shaft
beyond and below the horizontal at the top
of the swing. Ladies are the worst offenders,
perhaps because they hope to make up for
the weakness of arms and wrists by taking
the club well back and getting a longer swing.
But, instead of giving more power to the
stroke, the over-swing nearly always gives
rise to an orgy of mistiming. When swinging
the shaft up from behind the head and round
in so long a sweep, it is more difficult than
ever to time the action of the wrists and
make them snap through at the right moment.
The surest remedy lies in concentration on
keeping the elbows down as they are shown
in Plate VII.

Swaying is largely curable by perseverance
in keeping the head still. It is often due to
poor turning of the shoulders, a fault that
usually arises from knees too stiffly braced.
When addressing the ball the left knee should
not sag but it should certainly be relaxed.

Falling back when following through is another mistake as common as it is disastrous. The reason obviously lies in footwork. I have tried to make it clear that in carrying out the swing the weight is transferred from the right foot and left toe to left foot and right toe. When exactly the left heel comes to the ground it is difficult to say, but I gather from slow-motion pictures that it is at the actual moment of impact with the ball. If the whole of the left foot is not firmly on the ground at the follow-through, and the right heel raised, there is bound to be a leaning back of the body. So the player afflicted with a tendency to fall back must pay attention to his footwork.

Checking the club-head soon after impact is to many, apparently, a natural inclination. The least practical person should have no difficulty in realising that such a break in the swing is bound to shorten the length of a drive, and it breeds other evils that are not so obvious. Checking is more in the nature of a mannerism than a radical fault, and it is easily overcome by a little firmness and deliberate practice.

Pressing is a brother sin to checking, for both have common parentage in too tight a clenching of the club. The beginner at golf is often mystified by injunctions that he should not press, for it is the fault of the keen and over-anxious. It may be explained as hitting hard too soon : there is no limit to the strength of hitting the ball, but if this utmost force is exerted before its proper time the right shoulder drops too early and a poor drive follows. A watch must be kept on the pace of the club-head, moving slowly at first from the top of the swing and only reaching its maximum speed just as it meets the ball.

A spare moment is never wasted in practising the swing, whether it be upon a cork, a leaf or a blade of grass. As many of the necessary points as possible should be remembered, but especially the stance, the point of the swing in which the object should be struck and the direction in which the club-head should travel. There must be no stopping at impact, always a complete clean sweep. It is only by assiduous practice that an easy, natural swing can be obtained ; the many necessary rules can become so ingrained by constant use that they are followed mechanically, and the driver has nothing to disturb his concentration on a steady head and a good, free follow-through.

CHAPTER IV

THE BRASSIE

PLAY with the Brassie is never easy, but the extent of its difficulty depends upon the lie in the fairway. Even the best position must compare unfavourably with that on the tee ; a wooden club likes the ball to be well perched up above the ground, and this a Brassie rarely gets. No other club demands quite such skilful handling to connect the centre of its face with the centre of the ball.

Again, the Brassie is called upon to play the ball to a definite spot. It may be said that the drive is directed at the hole, but there is a vast difference between hitting one's hardest down the middle of the fairway and hitting definitely to the hole—neither beyond nor to the right or left. It takes a very short time to discover how much easier it is to stop a ball on the fairway than on the green.

The Brassie shot is nothing more than a long approach, and as such takes its place among the hardest strokes to play. I always advise exactly the same method as for the drive, in fact I prefer to use my Driver for the second shot unless there is doubt about picking the ball cleanly from the ground. The procedure, therefore, is as described in the previous chapter.

For the beginner, and for not a few others, there is a great temptation when playing with the Brassie to drop the right shoulder in an attempt to lift the ball by ducking at it. The careful watching of two points should counteract this : in the first place, the head must be kept quite still, not being allowed to drop forward, and secondly, the arms must bring the club back exactly as it addressed the ball. The sole of the club will brush the grass as it goes back and, if the shoulders are held at the proper level and the arms straight, will return to the ball in the same way. In connection with this second point of taking the club back from the ball along the ground I must be allowed a digression. It should not be difficult to realise that the longer the club-head keeps near the ground on its back swing the wider the arc of the drive is bound to be.

And the wider the arc the surer the player is of hitting the ball and following through in a straight line towards his objective.

Many players to-day, and almost everyone some years ago, set their backward swing into motion by a turn of the wrists that lifts the club from the ground behind the ball and

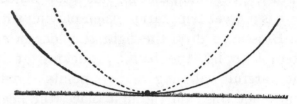

THE " HANDS FIRST " THEORY.

The unbroken line shows the wide arc described by the club-head when the " hands first " theory is practised ; the dotted line is the sharper arc resulting when the club is lifted straight up from behind the ball.

supplies the initial power in raising it. I believe it is to Vardon that we owe an advance on this state of affairs, for it was he who first practised, perhaps unconsciously, what has come to be known as the " hands first " theory. It was Vardon's custom, instead of turning his wrists to begin the stroke, to move his hands back before the club-head left its place behind the ball. The result was immensely important and for some considerable time peculiarly neglected. Whereas the average player in those days took his club straight off the ground going back and so perforce had to hit the ball absolutely exactly at the bottom of his swing, Vardon made his hands lead his club back and so caused its head to travel for some inches parallel to the ground.

The sweep of his drive was as it were flattened in the lowest part of its course, so that he was easily able to deal the ball a true blow and still enjoy an unprecedented margin for error. In effect, he could hit the ball with accuracy at any point within this flattened bottom section of his swing. True, the section was a short one, but even so it was infinitely preferable to the one and only point demanded by the commonly used acuter arc.

Just as the hands lead the club in taking it back, so too, to preserve the wide arc, they must precede it in coming down to the ball. The consequent action may be likened, with obvious qualifications, to the using of a flail or similar thrashing implement. In following through no one is going to believe that his

hands should lead the club. Where then does
the club-head pass the wrists ? The answer
contains the secret of genuine vital hitting
as distinct from the academically correct but
lifeless drive. Immediately before impact
the hands are ahead of the club, whereas the
moment the ball has been struck it is followed
by the club-head, now in front of the hands.
Clearly the change in the order of precedence
takes place at the crucial instant of hitting
the ball.

Presumably the hands do not check their
rapid sweep just as they bring the club-head
to the ball, yet this is when the latter passes
them. Plainly the speed of the club-head is
accelerated at the bottom of its swing to
enable it to get ahead. The added momen-
tum is supplied by a whipping action of the
wrists, giving highest speed as the ball is
struck. Such is the means of ensuring that
a true blow shall be dealt with the sting or
snap that everyone recognises and so many
are envious to possess.

Though perhaps I should be dealing here
strictly with the method of using the Brassie,
I take the liberty of discussing this " hands

first " theory in the belief that its interest and
its importance are equally great. More than
one scientist of the game, and notably Dr.
Gillies, who brought upon his ingenious head
the wrath of an outraged and sober-minded
authority by adopting a beer bottle as a
picturesque but effective tee, have busied
themselves with the problem of which part of
the body is the first to move in making a
stroke at golf.

It is now, I believe, generally accepted that
action commences with that pivoting which
I stressed so much in the last chapter and
which has its beginnings in the turning of the
hips. Following this line of argument we
arrive at the conclusion, contrary to all the
canons of a decade ago, that the club-head is
the last to move in beginning the stroke.
The turning of the hips leads off and creates
such bodily force as is communicated by way
of the shoulders to the arms and finally
through the wrists to the club-head. At first
sight it may appear that the old idea of getting
the arms and wrists into a shot is entirely
cancelled, but I believe I have made it amply
clear above that the " hands first " method,

on the contrary, accentuates the importance
of wrist-work to a degree hitherto uncon-
ceived.

To return to the Brassie. The fault of
ducking at the ball can be successfully coun-
tered and the general standard of play greatly
improved by assiduous practice in swinging
the club back close to the ground and
bringing it down in the same manner. When
the ball lies somewhat close and it is yet
thought that a Brassie shot should be
attempted, I would advise some slight modifications of stance. This should be so arranged
that the ball is rather nearer the centre of a
line between the feet ; an inch or two in this
direction makes a great deal of difference
when using a club that has little loft to its
face. But I repeat emphatically that there
is no more rash ambition or false heroism than
taking a club for a shot which really belongs
to the next in the bag. When, therefore, a
close lie in the fairway causes any hesitation
it will be well to take a Spoon and play for
safety.

CHAPTER V

THE SPOON

THE Brassie is a club for a short handicap player rather than the beginner, and in its place the Spoon is usually used. The two clubs are not actually interchangeable, and the plus man can find plenty of work for both, but there are probably many more people who fall back on the Spoon for a long shot through the green than there are users of Brassie and Spoon strictly for the shot for which they are intended.

The Spoon has a face that is rather more lofted or set back than the Brassie, and so it is far easier to lift the ball and get it cleanly away ; further, the face of the Spoon is shallower and so better suited for cutting beneath the ball.

It might be well to mention here the Baffy, a club so similar to the Spoon that I do not consider it worth a chapter to itself. The Baffy head is built on slightly different lines,

being unusually round in shape and having a
deeper face. But there is rarely any advantage in its use and, for myself, I have faith in
the sufficiency of Brassie and Spoon to follow
the Driver.

In skilful hands the Spoon can be made to
do many different things, but it will be enough
to deal mainly with the everyday straightforward shot ; more advanced work will be
attempted only by the first-class pro. or
amateur who is not in need of my instruction.
As far as possible, intentional pulling and
slicing are to be avoided ; except on rare
occasions even the greatest players are best
served by straightforward shots. In playing
with the Spoon it is well to take up a more
open stance (Plate IX) than when using
the Driver. The left heel is only about
two inches from the line of the ball. The
importance of " sitting down " on the ball is
greater in this case than most others ; the
knees should be pushed forward a little and
the right knee ought to bend rather more than
the left.

Plate V shows that the shaft does not
reach the horizontal at the top of the swing

by at least two inches : over-swinging is one of the greatest enemies of consistency and, unless overcome by perseverance and practice, will always mean erratic play. To arrive correctly at the finish it is necessary to observe all the rules of the swing. Since the beginner frequently imagines that it is supremely difficult to pick the ball from anything approaching a close lie with a wooden club, he will often dip his shoulders in a misguided attempt to get under the ball. If the head is kept perfectly still and the body freely pivoted there will be no difficulty in making a clean stroke. Any effort to lift the ball must be avoided ; the face of the club is lofted specially for this purpose and will do its work well enough if it is allowed. After it has hit the ball, the club-head should keep close to the ground for fully six inches of the follow-through.

When the lie is so close that a Spoon would seem risky it is probably wise to play for safety and take a No. I Iron, but there is no harm in practising difficult Spoon shots. Under such circumstances the stance is taken with both feet equidistant from the ball. If the balance is accurately kept this change will result in the club-head striking the ball before it has reached the lowest point in its swing and therefore taking a little turf. This is, in fact, an iron shot played with a wooden club.

The difficult Spoon shot thus played with a closed stance holds more than one snare for the unwary. Unless the stroke is timed with the greatest precision the ball will be smothered by a blow with the shut or turned-in face of the club. The effect of the shot on the other wooden clubs is, to say the least, unhealthy. The practice of hitting too much under the ball is a habit far more easily acquired than overcome, and it is for this reason that I invariably advise a pupil to take his No. I Iron for a ball that lies really close but in every other respect cries out for a Spoon.

Any change in stance or action with a particular club is undesirable, for it necessarily increases the amount of knowledge a player must possess and broadens the field for mistakes. Perfect golf is the using of the right club in the right way on each occasion.

From a close lie the ball can be taken with a natural No. I Iron shot, but the Spoon cannot be used without sundry modifications of method. There are two main points to bear in mind when using the Spoon : take a shorter swing than for a drive, with the head and body steady, and follow well through in a wide arc.

CHAPTER VI

THE NO. 1 IRON

In this book I have no chapter on the Cleek because it has been displaced to a large extent by the No. 1 Iron. Although this Iron is almost universally preferred there are still some who use the Cleek; to any such who read these pages I would say that there is no difference in treatment and that the actual playing of the shot is the same with either club. The clubs differ structurally in two respects, but even so the distinction is very slight. The No. 1 Iron is lofted a little more than the Cleek, and it is a trifle deeper in the face. These characteristics probably account for the increased popularity of the Iron, for they make it a comparatively easy club, whereas the Cleek has always been considered one of the most difficult with which to play. This difficulty is due chiefly to the extreme straightness of face which is a feature of the club and makes a clean shot from the fairway a matter of considerable skill. The general tendency to use the Spoon in preference to the Brassie is doubtless due to the same reason.

It is not unnatural that there should be improvement in a game so widely played as golf, and the disuse of the Cleek may, I think, be fairly called an improvement. The No. I Iron shot is considerably easier to play ; it can be used whenever a Cleek was previously taken, and there is no appreciable difference in the result. To play with a club that makes the game more difficult without corresponding advantage, when there is a simpler club to be used, is surely the height of folly. The extra loft on the face of the Iron is so slight that the flight and carry of the ball are not perceptibly affected, yet it is this extra loft that simplifies so much the execution of the stroke. Experience has shown me that I can hit a ball as far with a No. I Iron as with a Cleek, and I certainly have more confidence in the former club.

The feeling of complete confidence in one's clubs is an essential in good golf. A player cannot do himself justice if he feels ill at ease with any particular club. The elimination of all uncertainty is as necessary in this connection as it is in the co-operation of brain and body.   There must be no doubts or distractions to disturb that unruffled confidence which is so great a part of success in the game. If you feel surer of playing a good shot with your Cleek, then give away your No. I Iron ; but if, on the other hand, you are among the great majority who are more at ease with the Iron, do not attempt to use your Cleek.

There will always be a certain number of golfers who scoff at the possession of any club between a Spoon and a No. II Iron. I am convinced that such a club is essential for the player with a handicap of twelve and under, for it often happens that the lie of the ball and its position between tee and hole calls for a shot between these two clubs. If the bag contains no No. I Iron it means either pressing with the No. II, or sparing the Spoon. Quite apart from the general undesirability of playing any stroke otherwise than correctly, this fault of intentional exaggeration or restraint invariably affects the swing for subsequent shots.

Too much stress cannot be laid on the rule

of using a club well within its power. Each one is constructed for a particular style of shot, and none must be strained by attempting work which is really in the province of the club next above it in hitting strength. It is not the club which will suffer, but the stroke, if this rule is not observed. In theory, such advice seems hardly worth the giving, but there are many players who in practice tax their clubs beyond the task for which each is especially designed. It is to avoid this spoiling of No. II Iron and Spoon shots that I advocate the use of the intermediate No. I Iron.

For playing a ball up to the hole with this Iron from a good lie on the fairway, a stance is taken similar to that for a Spoon shot. The swing should be a good three-quarter, in which the club-head goes over the right shoulder until the shaft is nearly horizontal. The best guide is Plate XI. Here it will be seen that the shoulders and the left knee are in almost exactly the same position as in the corresponding stage of the drive (Plate IV). In both cases the upper part of the body is pivoted round from the hips to its full extent, so that the point of the left shoulder is immediately above the centre of a line between the feet. The position of arms and wrists should be noticed carefully. Both elbows are kept well down in order to give a compactness to the swing.

The downward swing and follow-through with the No. I Iron demand exactly the same action of arms, wrists, shoulders and knees as in use of the Driver. In both cases, the club-head meets the ball at the extreme point of its arc. Particular attention ought to be paid to the right shoulder and right knee in the follow-through; they should follow up the club-head in the line of flight. Balance is maintained through the left knee returning to its first position and taking rather the greater share of weight.

A want of balance spoils any shot and, unless the follow-through of the Iron is played correctly, mismanagement of the left leg will prove disastrous. The left foot must be squarely and firmly placed on the ground, the left knee straight. It will be found a great help to this end if the heel is not raised too much on the backward swing. A frequent mistake in the first stage of the shot is

to throw almost all the weight on to the right
foot, with merely the tip of the left toe on
the ground. From this position the preservation of balance through the downward swing
and follow-through is made a matter of
infinite difficulty. Plate VIII shows the left
heel raised just sufficiently to allow the knee
to come well in, and to assist in the turning of
the shoulders.

I will not say that excellent shots cannot be
made off the right foot, especially since the
introduction of the push shot, but I do believe
that the left heel should be allowed to take a
great deal more weight than is often the case.
It is very easy, too easy, to let the hands lead
the club when playing off the right foot; they
tend to pass the ball so much in front of the
club-head that a topped shot or a smother is
almost inevitable for any except the highly
skilled in wrist work. In the same way a
stance too far in front of the ball leads to
slicing and socketing—hitting the ball at the
joint of the face and the socket of the club-
head. It is much simpler, as well as more
effective, to play with the ball nearer the left
heel except in peculiar circumstances.

Another common error, offspring of faulty footwork, is checking the follow-through. This is due to holding the weight back on the right foot instead of transferring it as the ball is struck ; it astonishes me how few golfers employ their weight properly and to full advantage in using the Iron. Swaying on the back swing will also make it impossible to follow through with accuracy, necessitating a further swaying back into position and a considerable feat of balancing to get the weight on to the left foot at impact. On the other hand it is disastrous to overswing in the follow-through. I have seen numbers of players fling the club after the ball with such abandon and absence of control that the shaft has struck the shoulder.

The perfection of foot and knee action often takes a great deal of perseverance, but it is well worth the trouble. No one has attained a correct, easy and smooth action in this respect without a certain amount of drudgery. In this case, as always, persistent practice will be amply rewarded. There is a tendency among a few people to believe that a careful reading of such instructions as are given above is all that is required to produce a perfectly good stroke. If any beginner after learning the theory of the Iron shot can straightway go out and execute it faultlessly he will be a potential champion, for he is a natural golfer and the species is rare.

There is never a golfer so good that he can learn no more. The best of players are always looking out for some improvement, some means of increasing accuracy. The same principle should be present with still greater force in the beginner, for he must so practise that his mind shall be free of the responsibility of thinking of how he is producing his strokes. He must know and feel that mechanically he will do the best he is capable of, with scarcely any mental effort. This happy condition of mind is best achieved by studying each stroke in detail and especially such portions of the movement as present difficulty. Not otherwise can enjoyment or proficiency be attained.

The No. I Iron is not a club with which to take risks. It should never be used when there is any doubt about picking a ball cleanly off the ground. Far better to take the next

club, a No. II Iron, and make reasonably sure
of getting the ball well away. If the No. I
is chosen for a close lie, the stance should be
opened a little and the ball should lie exactly
between the feet. When actually hitting
such a ball the face of the club may be laid
slightly back, and a descending blow should
be struck ; turf is taken after impact, but the
follow-through must not be checked. It is a
shot to be played with the greatest care, for
the straightness of the face of the club gives
rise to much danger of smothering the ball.
A long handicap man indulging in such
adventures would be as a baby who tries to
run before he has learnt to walk.

The value of this club is greatly increased
and appreciated when playing in a wind.
Whether the enemy comes straight down the
fairway or across, the No. I Iron may be
freely used. Here, again, it is the individuality of the straight face that is concerned, for
the ball is kept low without any noticeable
difference in swing being a necessary preliminary. Under such circumstances it is
advisable to stand somewhat in front of the
ball, by which means the hands are slightly

in front of the club-head. Rather more
weight than usual is borne by the left toe at
the top of the swing, and the club face meets
the ball before the lowest part of the swing.
It is obviously more difficult to keep a steady
balance when playing the shot in this way, but
it is no less important that any suspicion of
sway or rockiness should be avoided. When
using the Iron in a wind it is useful to remember that a rather shorter back swing
makes for far better control of balance and
club. First and last, never should it be forgotten that the head must be kept quite still

CHAPTER VII

THE NO. II IRON

This club, often called the Mid-Iron, is a favourite of many players. It is the one with which they seem to have least difficulty in hitting the ball. To play really well with the No. II Iron is by no means easy, but any average player can perform with it passably well. Just as the No. I Iron is used by the less experienced in place of a Cleek, so this Iron is taken by those who have little confidence in their skill with the Spoon. The difference in face certainly makes it easier than the Spoon, and anyone is well advised to use it until he has sufficient confidence in his wooden clubs.

The No. II Iron allows, perhaps, a wider margin of error than any other club. Bad stance or imperfect wrist work may turn the face of the club in too much to the ball, and yet the resulting shot does not apparently suffer to the extent that it should; in such a

case even a little more length may be obtained
unintentionally. If a wooden club shot were
treated in this way the smaller degree of loft
would inevitably lead to bad smothering.
But this does not mean that the Mid-Iron is
to be taken up as a sort of light relief, in the
use of which all rules and points of style can
go by the board. There is, of course, a
correct way to play the club, and consistently
good results can only be the outcome of
skilful and practised handling.

Good use of this club is the hall-mark of a
first-class golfer, for there is a much more
noticeable difference in the Iron play of a
good and a moderate performer than there is
when the same players use wooden clubs.
The ball is not struck in the same way by the
Driver and Brassie as by the iron clubs : it
would be futile to analyse here the nicer
points of this distinction, and my purpose is
better served by fairly detailed instruction in
the use of the No. II Iron.

Both grip and stance vary from those
employed in most cases. The grip is firmer
than usual, and considerably tighter than
when wooden clubs are held. An under-

standing of the stance will be helped by reference to Plate X. It will be seen that the ball is nearer to the feet than usual, and that the right foot is a little in front of the left. The left toe is turned out considerably in the direction of the hole, while the ball lies exactly between the toes.

It should be noticed that—although the hands are a bit in advance of the club-head— ball, hands and nose are all in the same straight line. In order to keep the heel of the club well to the ground, both wrists are held down. If this were not observed, the face of the club could not meet the ball squarely, and a very imperfect shot would certainly follow. Although the arms are not allowed to hang loosely, but are kept firmly in position, yet the elbows must not be stretched taut. Stiffness of the arm at full length would obviously be the death of freedom and grace of style.

To allow the right shoulder to fall into a good striking position, the right knee should be a little more bent than the left. The weight is evenly distributed between the feet, falling within their span rather than upon them. It is always important to remember that the body should be supported well within the compass of the two feet ; any part which is outside the area they prescribe is a serious menace to stability and balance.

In the back swing the left knee and arm, and the shoulders, move together. The right elbow must be kept down ; many players find a tendency to lift it with a view to obtaining more power, but especially with the Mid-Iron must this temptation be resisted. At the top of the swing an upward movement of the wrist levers the club-head over the right shoulder. Here, again, a certain degree of restraint must be exercised. Plate XI shows the club at the top of a *full* swing with the No. II Iron, and it will be noted that the shaft is still some way from the horizontal. A very common fault is this levering over of the head of the Iron too far behind the head, and it must be carefully guarded against until the correct swing has become instinctive.

To complete the action of the swing with this club the order is reversed. The left arm and knee, and the shoulders, move together, and the wrists are straightened out as the

club-head nears the ball. The whipping with
the wrists begins a little earlier than in the
case of the Driver, for instance, because the
Iron must strike before it has reached the
lowest point of its swing. Downward movement of the club-head is, of course, continued
a little after impact with the ball, but in
taking turf there must be no break in the
smooth turning of the shoulders.

Care must be taken in the follow-through
that the weight is not thrown outside the
area of its support. In Plate XII, illustrating
the finish, the entire weight of the body is
seen to be well behind the left foot. A careless hitter will often over-reach the limit and
fall forward, with grievous consequences for
the ball, the course on which he is playing,
and even for his club. The complete turn
of the shoulders is within the radius indicated
by the toes.

The club-head is made to follow through
in a direct line to the hole by keeping the
right arm straight until the shoulders have
come full circle and the swing is almost
ended. The left arm acts in the follow-
through exactly as did the right during the

backward swing; the same care must be taken to keep the elbow pointing downward and the arm into the side. On the other hand, any suggestion of cramping will show at once that something is dismally wrong.

Learning to play golf is much like learning to dance : at first there is a rather troublesome period during which concentration must be made upon footwork, position and movement. Gradually the rules are kept and instructions followed without any conscious effort. Finally comes the time when real enjoyment proves how much worth while were the somewhat less pleasant hours spent in learning.

CHAPTER VIII

THE JIGGER

UNTIL a few months ago I had never used this club. I was in the habit of carrying two Mashies, one a powerful weapon with so straight a face that it approached a No. II Iron, while the other conformed to the regular Mashie type, having its face laid well back for lofting. Then one day I broke my straight-faced Mashie. There was nothing in my shop of the same sort, so for the first time I took out a Jigger and tried it seriously. After a little practice I found that it gave better results than my old Mashie, and ever since then it has been very useful in many circumstances.

The Jigger is intended for use between the No. II Iron and the Mashie, being in construction a compromise of both. My heavy Mashie with the straight face was a Jigger in almost everything but name, and I am convinced that it was right to discard it for

a club that has distinct individuality and a
definite place in the bag. Instead of slogging
away with a Mashie at distances of 90 yards
and over, it is far better to use the Jigger.
No thinking golfer has any doubt about the
injury done to one's game by trying to get
more length than any particular club is built
to give. Overstraining with the Mashie, for
example, means that the swing becomes more
like that used for the Driver; consequently
it is found increasingly difficult to carry out
the regular short Mashie shots with accuracy
because overswinging causes slack and incorrect hitting.

The stance for playing with the Jigger
varies greatly, according to the nature of the
lie and the length of shot demanded. It is
almost always used for a forcing shot of some
description, and in such a case the player
should take up his position well forward with
the ball close to the right foot. With this
stance not only greater power and length will
result, but also the ball will be kept lower.
Such play gives a club hard wear, and for this
reason the purchaser of a Jigger should see
that he buys a stiff shaft; the head, too,

should be fitted with an upright lie so that it will be soled from toe to heel when used by a player standing close over the ball.

The Jigger is invaluable for fighting a head wind. Everyone knows how difficult it is to control a Mashie shot in such a situation : the ball seems determined to soar gracefully into the air, making little or no headway. Some circumstances allow the use of a Mashie against the wind, played with a very forward stance, but it is rarely possible to use the club successfully for long approaches in the face of anything more than a breeze. Without running the risk of being associated with the no doubt necessary but nevertheless tiresome company of golfing mathematicians, I can state as a fact that a Mashie shot invariably goes away with considerable back spin and therefore has the tendency to rise. To counteract the effects of head wind it is imperative that the spin, if any, should be in the opposite direction, and it is because the Mashie is totally unable to cope with such a situation that the Jigger becomes invaluable on a rough day.

Even when used with the firmness and

precision of a J. H. Taylor, the Mashie always tends to put the ball at the mercy of the wind, whereas the Jigger with its greater weight and closer face hits a ball that will bore through the most formidable of aerial obstacles. Although much is due to the nature of the club, it must not be forgotten that the chief factor ensuring low flight is the playing of a shot with the stance well up to the ball and in front of it. When the wind is behind, the ball should be opposite the left heel of the stance and the follow-through as low and long as possible.

If you cannot watch good golfers in action, get photographs of their stances and study them till they are part of your golfing nature. To try to follow through like Vardon if you do not stand as he does is more than useless—it is impossible.

But I have wandered from the immediate matter in hand, my advocacy of the Jigger. Many of my pupils fail to realise that the Jigger shot is much the same as that played with the Mashie, and they tend to deal full-blooded Iron hits rather than the pushing-through stroke. To correct this fault I let

them take a ball in the hand and roll it along
the ground as in the game of bowls : they
then have to apply this action to their stroke,
the club-head taking the place of the hand
and the stance not dissimilar. The club is
pushed hard through the ball, as it were, and
follows it up at arm's length.

If the reader has no Jigger in his bag,
regarding it as an unnecessary freak, let him
take the advice of a convert and straightway
make a purchase he is never likely to regret.

CHAPTER IX

THE Mashie is a difficult club to master because it is called upon to do so much. No other club has to deal with such a variety of strokes, differences in stance and swing being demanded by all manner of lies. It is always expected of the Mashie that it will pitch the ball on to the green, if not near the hole, and in doing this it is constantly faced with different situations : the ball in a hole or on a mound, behind a bank or on a slope, badly in the rough or sitting up on the fairway. Good play with this club, therefore, depends largely on ability to adapt style to circumstance.

There are many badly-constructed Mashies to be seen on every course ; some have as much loft as a Niblick and others are almost straight in the face. As always, the extreme is to be avoided and a medium loft preferred : the club should combine the features necessary to obtain reasonable length as well as suitability for picking the ball up cleanly from its lie.

I will describe first the method of playing a straightforward full Mashie shot from the fairway with no intervening bunker, the use of the club under best possible conditions. The stance is illustrated in Plate XIII. The right foot is parallel to the line running between the feet at right angles to the line of flight, while the left is further back, and well turned out towards the hole ; both are the same distance from the ball. The position of arms and shoulders is of first importance. The left shoulder and the club-head are about as far apart as they can be, yet the left arm points between the feet rather than at the ball. This ensures the keeping of the left elbow close in to the body.

Since the ball is struck in the downward swing, it should lie fairly close to the right foot. The most necessary feature of a correct swing back is firmness and straightness of the left arm, and this is maintained by proper turning of the shoulders and bending of the left knee. The knee moves fully as much as the shoulders, and it is especially difficult for the learner to keep his left foot in correct position ; the foot must not turn, but the heel should leave the ground very slightly, pressure falling on the inside of the big toe. The value of a photograph of the top of a swing taken from behind the ball is that it shows more clearly the part played by wrists and forearms.

Overswinging is probably the commonest of all Mashie faults. The swing with this club is essentially a compact one. The easiest way to contract the overswing habit is to let the elbows swing away from the sides, so its remedy should be clear. Another prevailing evil is the shut face that is adopted in the hope of gaining length : but it is accuracy and not length that should be looked for in Mashie play. An open stance and shoulders well turned to the front must accompany the open face, otherwise the club will not be square to the hole and a slice will follow. A closed face is often caused unconsciously by faulty grip, the right hand being too much beneath the shaft. If the swing is carried out entirely by the wrists, or if the left arm is allowed to check its movement at the moment of impact, a stab will follow. The club-head must swing smoothly through as it hits the ball, not bury itself in the ground.

The actual shot includes both ball and turf in the sweep, the wrists forcing the club through in an unbroken swing to take first the ball and then the turf. At the finish the position is the reverse of that at the top of the swing, but the wrists are still beneath the shaft. Throughout the movement the left arm is the controlling and directing power, while the wrists straighten out just before the bottom of the swing to deliver the blow. When the regular full Mashie shot can be played consistently well the playing of the shorter shots becomes a much easier proposition.

For a short shot off the fairway the uninitiated, and not a few others, imagine that the same length of swing with a slacker movement will meet the case. Early disaster should disillusion them. The whole mechanism for hitting the ball must move in exactly the same way as before, except that there is a shorter swing back : the action of striking is as crisp as any full shot. In such a case the club-head should not be allowed to

travel higher than the wrist line when
following through ; the elbows are still in
to the sides and the shaft points straight at
the hole, while the face of the Mashie is half
to the sky and half to the left.

One of the greatest pleasures of using this
very pleasant club is that of pitching a ball
on to the green so that it stops as nearly as
possible dead. To do this it is necessary to
modify the stance by bringing the right foot
forward and letting the left drop back until
it is opposite the ball. The outcome of such
a change is the most open of all stances,
permitting a very upright swing with the club.
The club face is turned out to an extent that
would certainly give rise to a bad slice if
played in the ordinary way. But the exceedingly open stance brings the shoulders round
until they face the hole almost squarely, and
this new position counteracts the turning of
the face. Any player who finds that his
Mashie shots under these conditions seem
regularly drawn away to the right should
alter the position of his feet and make his
stance more open.

The stance itself causes an upright swing

and the club comes down to the ball at a much more acute angle than in the straightforward shot, so chopping the ball as to create the necessary back-spin. At the finish of the swing, out in front of the player, the face of the club is turned upwards and the right wrist is directly beneath the shaft.

For a ball lying close to the ground, in an awkward depression or similar bad lie, an open stance is again taken, but not in so exaggerated a form as for the pitch shot. The swing is unchanged except that the hands come down slightly ahead of the club-head, and so give a steeper angle to the shot. It is important when playing under such circumstances to remember that the full face of the blow must fall on the ball and not on the ground behind it. On the other hand, there is equal danger of stabbing, striking the club into the ground instead of following through and taking turf immediately after impact. The fault is most commonly caused by swaying or leaning too far forward, an easy enough defect to remedy.

The ordinary short pitch and run shot on to the green from about twenty yards does

not call for any lifting of the left heel, because
the swing is short. But it is easy to go too
far in the other direction and restrict knee
movement as well, which is fatal. Sufficient
give at the knees is essential to good timing
of the swing, the left knee moving as the club
goes back and the right with the follow-
through. Again, no good results can come
from purely wrist action in using the Mashie ;
as the wrists turn, the left arm must move
back to an extent governed by the length of
shot demanded.

For all strokes with the Mashie, under
every circumstance, the movement required
is the same. Real skill in using the club lies
in ability to moderate the several parts of this
movement in proper proportion as each case
demands. An absolute essential is a firm
left wrist, its function similar to that of a
strong spring which is allowed no loose
movement.

CHAPTER X

BEFORE the rubber-cored ball was adopted very few players knew of this club, but in recent years it has grown rapidly in favour. With the new ball it was discovered that better control in approaching was often obtained with a Niblick than with a Mashie, owing to the higher flight and greater amount of back spin that the former club imparts. A Niblick, however, is too much lofted to give any real length, so a club was designed on the same lines as the Niblick but having less loft to its face. This naturally took its place between Mashie and Niblick, and was named accordingly.

The value of the Mashie Niblick is most appreciated when a shot is required not only to surmount a bunker, but also to carry some little distance ; a Mashie would give sufficient length and a Niblick would carry the bunker, but only a combination of the two clubs can deal adequately with such a shot. It is not surprising that many golfers improve their game a great deal by using a Mashie Niblick, for it gives them better control over the ball in a certain type of approach shot and fills a legitimate place in the bag.

It is necessary to follow a correct procedure if the club-maker's work is to be of benefit. An open stance best suits the straightforward Mashie Niblick stroke : the right foot at right angles to the line of flight and the left toe turned outwards. The ball should be opposite the left heel. Both plates XIV and XV, illustrating this club, show the elbows well into the sides ; this is important for a satisfactory approach, and it also necessitates the position of the ball close to the toes. This attitude is not at all comfortable at first, but it is essential for such work, and practice soon dispels any feeling of awkwardness.

As in the case of the Mashie, so here the back swing has to be compact and not too full; Plate XV shows its maximum, with elbows still close and wrists beneath the shaft. When the club is taken back there should be

a distinct pressure on the left toe, and if the
heel is raised at all its movement must be
severely restricted.   Personally I ease my
left heel just enough to allow my weight to be
on the toe.   If this rule is observed there will
be less danger of swaying, the bugbear of all
such shots.

The club-head strikes its blow while it is
still coming down, and goes on to take turf
and to finish its swing without any more
interruption than is absolutely unavoidable.
It is more difficult to hit the ball deliberately
before the bottom of the swing is reached than
it is to play it in the orthodox way at the full
extent of the sweep with the club ; scrupulous
care must be taken, therefore, to preserve the
requisite balance.   The left arm should be
kept taut throughout the movement, for any
slackness will spoil the chances of accurate
timing ; it is a good plan to tighten the grip
with the left hand, so bracing the muscles of
the forearm and communicating its effect to
the whole limb.

A high shot is obtained by opening the face
of the club and aiming somewhat to the left
of the hole.   A lower trajectory is the result

of closer stance and the club face turned in.
In both cases the swing and method of
striking the ball are exactly the same. Footwork and swing must become so instinctive
through practice that all the attention may
be concentrated on bringing the club face
properly to the ball.

CHAPTER XI

THE NIBLICK

OF all the clubs the Niblick is probably the most neglected. How few people there are who go out with a Niblick alone, to practise shots which will get them out of difficult places. I know one man who did so, and he has reaped a rich reward for his pains. He now has full confidence in the club, bunkers have lost much of the terror they used to hold for him, bad lies near the green no longer present great difficulty. Why the Niblick is not practised is in the nature of a mystery to me, for it is as much used as any of the clubs, and most often its work is of highly critical importance.

If the club is properly mastered it will save more strokes in a round than would have been thought possible by anyone who had not closely and practically examined its value. The advantages it offers do not lie solely in helping the ball from a tight corner, but very largely in its influence upon the nerves and composure of its user. The word " psychological " has been made responsible for so much in recent years that it may well be threadbare ; nevertheless it is a matter of definite fact that the effect of good play with the Niblick is, above all, psychological.

A man who is master of his Niblick does not go into the bunker with the hopeless air of one already beaten. He is not put off his shot by fear of missing—a state of affairs which inevitably turns the fear into an accomplished fact. Instead, he plays out as well as the lie allows, using his Niblick to the best advantage, because practice has given him not only skill in its use but also the supremely important factor of confidence. In dealing with a ball in an awkward position it is no less important to know the best way to play it than it is to execute the stroke correctly.

I know of no shot that gives more pleasure than one well played from a bunker, or a lift over a hazard with the Niblick : after such achievements one feels that something has been accomplished. A good drive gives much pleasure—but then a drive should be good,

for it is made under ideal conditions. The
Niblick has not to deal with a ball teed upon
a specially prepared piece of ground, it is used
under very different circumstances.

The most difficult aspect of Niblick play is
the stance ; it varies on almost every occasion
that the club is used. According to the
position of the ball it may be necessary to
have one leg much above the level, or perhaps
lower than usual ; the whole stance may have
to be taken at an unaccustomed height above
the ball, or the reverse may be demanded.
The only infallible rule is that the feet shall
be so placed and the body so disposed that
the ball may be struck truly with the centre
of the club-face. The taking up of stance,
always according to fixed plan in other cases,
is here left to the judgment of the individual.
It is easy to realise that, under such circumstances, practice is of paramount importance.

Except in a few cases, with which I will deal
later, the Niblick always strikes the ball a
descending blow while it is still on its downward swing. To illustrate an average Niblick
shot I will suppose the ball lying on the fairway close behind a bunker which is some little

distance from the flag. The feet take the same position as for the Mashie, with the ball lying exactly midway between them. The club should be taken straight back, the right elbow being held well into the side, and should be lifted at the end of the back swing by an upward bending of the wrists.

At the top of the swing—which must not be too long—the left knee is bent in towards the ball, but the heel remains firmly on the ground. The left arm should be held straight and almost exactly horizontal, at the height of the waist-line. As in most other strokes, the right elbow must be kept close to the side, but in this stroke it points to the rear rather than downwards.

Much of the work of the downward swing is done by the wrists. They force the club-head down and keep it low on a direct follow-through, being assisted by the straight right arm. Throughout the stroke the club is guided by the left arm, which is held straight until the finish, when it may be allowed to bend in rounding off the follow-through. The left elbow must not be given more freedom than the right—in fact it is a good rule to keep both elbows as close to the sides as is possible without cramping.

Control of strength in playing a ball with the Niblick is of some importance, for such shots are demanded at a wide range of distances. The wrists and the right forearm regulate the strength of pitch and run by giving the requisite amount of speed to the downward swing of the club-head.

There are, of course, many more difficult lies than one in the fairway immediately behind a bunker. In playing from rough grass it is advisable to stand a little in front of the ball. Impact is again made on the downward swing, but with more pressure on the club-head. The grip must be tight, and any semblance of stabbing at the ball is to be avoided. A widespread notion is that the lie in long grass demands merely a thrust at the back of the ball, without any attempt at follow through. It is rarely possible to cut right through and finish the swing, but this should always be the ambition. A stroke which is intended to end as soon as the ball has been struck is bound to suffer before it reaches the crucial point.

Any shot in the rough must be played with the intention of getting the face of the club to the ball quickly and cleanly. It is to avoid undue hacking at grass behind the ball that the stance is taken a little forward. The club face should be open during the swing, which means that it is turned outwards. The stance must be opened, too, the shoulders being turned almost squarely to the hole.

In playing from a difficult lie there is often a tendency to sway, in the belief that a manœuvring of the body during the stroke will make up for an awkward stance. This is a fatal mistake that cuts across all the accepted principles of the game ; it seems the natural way of making the best of an unpleasant position, but actually it makes matters infinitely worse. However rough the ground or steep the slope, a player must always aim at secure stance and a good grip with the feet. Hastiness seldom pays for the time it saves, and a little consideration invariably discovers the firmest position in which to play the ball without having to contort the body. The actual hitting with a Niblick is always with the forearm and wrists ; these are helped to function to the best advantage by correct movement of the shoulders, but they do not derive any driving power from the upper part of the body.

When playing out of sand, an open stance is again adopted. The club-head is laid square with the hole and driven into the sand an inch behind the ball : it passes under the ball and lifts a quantity of sand as well. There is no checking of the swing and, again, any suspicion of stab is avoided. The feet may be worked well into the sand to secure a sure hold, which is as necessary as the subsequent firm grip and forceful blow. Neither foot is moved or lifted, but kept as rigorously still as the head.

A little practice and a little success will clear away the attitude of mind that connects the Niblick with all the difficulties of the game and none of its delights. Too often it is taken up to stem a fierce current of expletives and is applied to the unhappy ball in a manner which implies that any whip is good enough to beat such a dog. At the same time there is in the club no especial virtue which itself retrieves a desperate position.

Practice alone will bring with it a proper appreciation of the truth that the pleasure of succeeding in an apparently hopeless position is worth several strokes more than its face value.

CHAPTER XII

PUTTING

THE putt is the easiest golf stroke to learn, and it is as important as any. A beginner is often apt to think that the missing of a simple putt is but a small thing compared with a foozled drive; yet the one is as expensive as the other. This disproportionate view is due, perhaps, to the fact that a bad putt seems a mistake on a small scale. But it is none the less costly for that, and, because it is so easily learnt, there is comparatively little excuse.

Putting is almost half the game of better players. That this is not merely a loose application of a figure of speech may be proved by practical analysis. It will be found that roughly one half of the total number of strokes by a good golfer in playing a round are putts. There is much to be learnt and practised before such efficiency between tee and green is possessed, but even in the earlier stages the importance of the putt must not be belittled.

Besides being the easiest of strokes to learn—which does not mean that it is the easiest to play—the putt probably allows more variety of style than is permissible in the use of any other club. Everyone has peculiarities and particular mannerisms which make up his individuality. These personal tendencies almost always run counter to the essential rules of golf, but it is unwise to curb them altogether. The chief weakness of theories in any game is that they aim at pressing all players into a mould of the same shape. They do not allow for the personal factor. Such a state of affairs would be more nearly tolerable, perhaps, if the shape of the mould were always the same. But, though all theorists endeavour to turn out their victims according to pattern, in each case invariably it is a different pattern. If there are so many standards of correct play, surely personality may be allowed some measure of consideration. And it is in putting that a leavening of originality can be allowed with least danger of immediate disaster.

There are, however, certain main points which underlie good putting. They may be modified or garnished in accordance with personal taste, but once the individual has a satisfactory method it should not be varied. In the early stages of his game a player may experiment with many different styles of using his putter; having discovered that style which gives him the best results, he would be well advised to stick to it and to concentrate on its perfection.

I have tried numerous plans of action on the green with varying success. Nowadays I always putt in that way which experience has shown to give the best results. I will describe it in some detail, in the belief that its main principles will bring success to any who have the inclination and perseverance to model their own style upon it.

The stance is taken with the right foot exactly at a right angle to the line between ball and hole; the left toe is turned well round in the direction of the hole. The weight of the body, being evenly distributed on both feet, sinks down upon them in a manner more relaxed than in any other stance. Both knees are bent forward, but the right one sags rather further than the left in order to turn the body towards the hole. For the same reason, the left foot falls a little behind the right. Whatever individual alterations may be made in putting, it is well to keep hard and fast to the rule that the heels should not be more than six inches apart. It is imperative to get a clear and direct view of the line that the ball is to follow, and this is impossible when a wide stride is taken. The left heel should be in a position immediately opposite the ball and at that distance which gives the best view of the line of travel.

I cannot emphasise too strongly my conviction that the face of the putter should meet the ball squarely. There have been writers on the game who have discussed at great length and with admirable mathematical ability the advantages of " drag," " undercut," and " top-spin " in putting. They have exhausted many printed pages and the patience of still more readers. I imagine that the ambition of everyone who reads this book is to play a good game of golf. When that

ambition has been fulfilled will come the time
for indulging in cutting and spinning the ball
on the green. But a good game is most
easily acquired by perfection in the simpler
rules, of which the square face of the putter
is one.

If the face of the club is to stand at a
perfect right angle some attention must be
paid to grip and the position of the arms.
In squaring the club-head to the line I use
the same grip as with other clubs. The left
elbow turns a little towards the hole, sufficiently to tighten the left wrist against the
right, but not enough to give rise to uncomfortable lack of balance. In the case of the
right arm, the elbow is moved back until it
is in one and the same straight line as the
right hand and the hole.

When a correct and, above all, a comfortable stance has been obtained, the head of the
putter should be taken back with a smooth
and steady action of the wrists. It must
travel straight back from the ball, close to the
ground. The length of backward swing depends upon the distance of the putt, but it is
better to swing too short than too far behind.

The club-head falls against the ball with the same steady swing, the wrists straighten, and the follow-through shadows the ball in the direction of the hole. There must be no quickening of the stroke as the putter strikes the ball. It is not a hit, but more in the nature of a pendulum swing, which carries the ball with it. Head and elbows remain motionless throughout the whole action, for only thus can the ball be met exactly as it was addressed. A still head means steady shoulders, and the tendency to sway is much increased when there is so narrow a stance. Steadiness of the elbows prevents another powerful tendency—a rolling of the wrists which is bound to react on the club-face.

That part of the ball further from the hole should be watched intently from the first moment of addressing. The club-head is not seen except at the actual moment of meeting the ball. The danger of a wandering eye is much greater in putting than in longer shots, and especially when the putt is short. This is due to the nearness of ball and hole, and a consequent unconscious effort to embrace both in one glance. Many a putt is missed through watching the hole out of the corner of the eye for the pleasure of seeing the ball go down.

If the hands are allowed to move in front of the club-head a certain amount of spin will be imparted to the ball and its course will not be true. Any twisting or rolling of the wrists has a greatly magnified effect upon the face of the club, and a pushing forward of the hands is bound to react upon the wrists and consequently upon squareness of face.

There are so many different styles of putting all obtaining good results that it is difficult to say that any one is better than another. There is, however, one style which I have never known to pay : that is the sharp lifting of the club-head on the backward swing. It is a common fault and one that a good many players possess unconsciously. Analysis shows that in this case the club-head must go off the direct line to the hole. If such a putt be played along a chalk line, and the swing back be carefully watched, it will be seen that when the club-head is lifted sharply from behind the ball it moves over to the opposite side of the line to the player. With such a preliminary the striking of the ball is a matter of pure chance. To remedy this defect the club-head should be kept close to the ground going back; it must not be dragged, but swung freely by the wrists, both elbows being still. Much good will come of practice on such a line as I have referred to, and a straight swing so played will soon become natural.

When putting on an undulating green, I step behind the ball and consider the amount of deflection necessary to counteract slope. The eye fixes on a spot from which it is thought the ball will roll out of its course into the hole, and the putt is made in strength and direction with that spot as its objective. It is a well-known fact, one that the beginner soon discovers for himself, that it always pays to exaggerate the angle at which the putt is made in relation to the hole on uneven greens. To " borrow plenty " is far better than to make the shot " too narrow." When the amount of fall in a slope on the green is underestimated the ball invariably overruns the hole.

I believe that the best putting is achieved when an aluminium putter is used. Less effort is demanded in playing the shot, and there is an absence of jerk in consequence. Another of my contentions is that the sole of the club should be flat on the ground in addressing the ball. I am convinced that the line to the hole can be better judged when the eye is not too much over the ball.

In such a delicate stroke, steadiness of hand counts for much. Nervousness is the most general and the most charitable explanation of shakiness in this respect. It is an unfortunate and seemingly unfair handicap that one player should be more afflicted with nerves than another, and his weakness is naturally accentuated when he sets himself to play what is often the deciding stroke of the hole. But even the worst trembler can overcome his drawback by practice ; he can banish lack of confidence by showing himself repeatedly that he has the ability to do the right thing. Nervousness has every encouragement in green play : the shot is frequently a critical one, there is an atmosphere of expectancy and criticism which is felt only too easily, and the necessity for almost complete muscular relaxation forbids any bracing of the system.

In brief : gain confidence through practice, keep as steady and still as possible, swing the club-head close to the ground, and let all the action be smooth.

CHAPTER XIII

LENGTH AND HOW TO GET IT

IN writing about the Driver I emphasised
my belief that the satisfaction of long hitting
was in no way justified unless the flight of
such balls was effectively controlled. It
would be idle to deny the fascination of
hitting a long ball, but it would be quite as
illogical to set distance above direction.

Even when two players are driving straight
down the middle of the fairway one must out-
drive the other by at least thirty or forty
yards if he is to have any real advantage.
Indeed, I would rather lie just behind my
opponent than twenty yards ahead of him,
for then I have the opportunity of getting
a good shot in first and making the other man
play up to me instead of following his own
game. Many times I have seen this happen
to the ultimate advantage of the player who
in the first place drove the shorter ball.

One of the most obvious tactics of the long

hitter is to lead his opponent into pressing to keep up with him. No player who can keep his head should be perturbed by this treatment; he should realise that if he is unable to keep up by means of his ordinary swing it would be more than foolish to try to add twenty yards to his length at a minute's notice. On such occasions we make resolutions to practise long hitting with patience so that the same player will not lead us round when next we meet. These resolutions, and others like them, are rarely kept, otherwise there would be a very general shortening of handicaps. The effort is well worth making, and for such as are prepared to try with reasonable patience to develop greater length I will explain briefly my own methods in this connection.

In the first place, I would emphasise once more the often proved truth that weight and size have little to do with distance in driving. Wiry forearms and supple wrists are more to be valued than great strength, as is well exemplified by Mr. Roger Wethered and Michael Bingham, the Midland professional. Neither of them are heavily built men; on the contrary, both are of decidedly slim physique. Mr. Wethered and Bingham can drive as far as Abe Mitchell, but I would not for a moment suggest that either is so great a driver. Mitchell beats everyone for consistent combination of length and accuracy. Unfortunately I was never privileged to see Vardon at his best, but I should imagine that he and Mitchell are the greatest long and straight hitters that have ever played the game.

Because the factors of weight and size enter so little into these calculations, it must not be assumed that pure strength is at a discount. The strong player is able to give his club-head the requisite speed at the bottom of its swing without that additional and exaggerated effort that very frequently spoils the smoothness of a weaker man's drive. This ease in hitting does not necessarily add length to a shot, but it certainly does make for far greater sureness and regularity in keeping the ball under control.

In explaining the actual procedure which I believe to be responsible for length in driving, I shall not be misunderstood if I describe the

results of my own experience and the manner
of driving by which—although not above the
average physique—I have taught myself to hit
as long a ball as most.   It is not idle to repeat
here the advice given in Chapter III upon the
desirability of correct stance and balance.
Without these elementary necessities it is
quite out of the question to expect any of the
features of good driving, length among them.

If it can be said that there is such a thing
as the secret of length in golf—most writers
on the game seem to have some secret, chiefly,
perhaps, because they are anxious to tell it—
I should say that it lies in the striking position
or position at the top of the swing.   At this
stage the left shoulder ought to be opposite
the ball and the weight well balanced between
right foot and left toe.   The wrists must be
under the shaft, not only because this is the
position from which they can best do their
work, but also because they govern the
equally important action of the elbows.   On
no account should the shaft fall below the
horizontal : effort will have to be used to
raise it and will in proportion detract from
the power applied to the downward swing.

Assuming that a correct striking position has thus been obtained, the second part of the journey commences. The aim now is to get speed, great speed, into the swing of the club-head and yet preserve an effortless and unruffled action. Only perfect co-operation and harmony of wrists and shoulders can produce the smooth effect that is essential to good hitting. Almost as if it were a flail the club comes down to the ball, shoulders turning smartly and wrists whipping the club-head through. To sweep the club round so rapidly through three-quarters of a circle before striking, it is clear that the wrists must move very quickly indeed. Never should there be any pulling with the left arm; instinctively one feels that it will give strength to the stroke if the club-head is made by the arms to beat at the ball, instead of sweeping it easily from the tee. This is one of the instincts that has to be suppressed. The arms come down with the turn of the shoulders, just as they went up from the address. The left heel must also regain its position firmly at the moment of impact. Time and again I see players neglecting the importance of getting the left heel to the ground; their weight is not properly transferred and nearly half their natural power is lost. The downward swing should be in every way a replica of the swing back, and the transferring of weight is as essential as any other part of the movement.

As the head of the club goes through the ball it is followed quickly by the right shoulder and knee, a necessary preliminary to a good follow-through. The actual blow is delivered by the wrists, important as is the co-ordination of other parts of the body. Rough attention to these points and to the movement unbroken by impact will perhaps produce a drive of average length, but the player who is anxious to carry really well from the tee will study and practise them with the closest care.

The two important phases of action for long driving are well illustrated in Plates VII and the frontispiece, showing the striking position and the finish respectively. Better even than an intelligent examination of these photographs is the watching of first-class players: notice carefully the speed they get coming through the ball, and try to detect the smart turn of the shoulders from top of the swing to finish.   See how the power is generated by wrist work aided by perfect pivoting of shoulders from the hips.   Too hurried a raising of the club to the striking position will mean jerkiness, and too slow a back swing will result in stiffness of action : in either case length will suffer as much as accuracy.   As shown in the diagram accompanying Chapter III, the club-head must on no account swing outside the line of flight; a direct hit alone can give the maximum benefit of effort.

Finally, I would return to the main theme of this chapter—wrist work. The slightest misjudgment here and the face of the club will not connect properly with the ball—either it will be at the wrong angle, or it will not be travelling in the correct arc.

CHAPTER XIV

PULLING AND SLICING

It is a very open question whether it pays a player to learn to pull and to slice, and it is almost as doubtful whether there is ever much advantage in employing such strokes. Occasionally a situation may arise in which it seems desirable to drive a ball other than straight, but no one should attempt to learn how to pull or slice his ball intentionally until he has learnt how to avoid doing so accidentally.

There must be few who do not know to their cost how easy it is to slice, and everyone realises the difficulty of controlling the stroke. I am well aware that more than one writer has strongly denounced any neglect of spin, holding that the " plain-ball " game will carry a man no further in golf than it does in cricket and tennis. But in these two games only the specialist concerns himself with spinning the ball, and the same holds true in golf.

This book is intended rather to develop sound play than to ensure a plus player becoming Open Champion, and therefore a chapter on pulling and slicing is included with the emphasised qualification that it should not be studied seriously until a high degree of certainty and steadiness has been reached in straight driving. In Chapter II reference has been made to the part played by grip in directing the flight of the ball. A change of grip is the chief factor in playing these two indirect strokes, and it will be well to examine the position of the hands on the club in some detail.

In order to effect a slice the backs of both hands are turned more towards the hole than in the case of the straightforward stroke : the knuckles of the left hand face the hole almost squarely, while the right hand is pressed over against the left until it is practically on the top of the shaft. It will now be felt that both arms have lost much of their power if the ball is to be hit with the full face of the club. To strike with full force when the club is held in this grip the hands must twist to the right, turning the club-face outwards with them.

The turning of the wrists is unconsciously made so that the arms and upper part of the body may play their customary parts in the stroke.

It is obviously useless to think of executing a slice until the correct, straight swing has become second nature. Both strokes demand the same movements, and the slice depends for its effectiveness upon an instinctive determination to hit the ball with a maximum amount of power. When the club-head is speeding up just before impact in a true swing the wrists automatically find their strongest position. If this is so and if a grip has been taken for slicing, the wrists will at the last moment bring the club-face against the ball at an angle. The slice is caused, of course, by this striking of a glancing blow. A correct judgment of the amount of slice to be given can only be the result of practice. The grip is taken as I have described and the shot is aimed at a spot to the left of the hole ; after this has been practised several times it will have become clear how much deviation is caused by the rearranged grip in any individual case. This method of playing for a slice calls for no alteration in the general rules beyond changed grip and an aim to one side of the hole.

There is another method which has been touched upon in the latter part of the chapter on the Drive. This is slicing by means of the open stance, the left foot having been

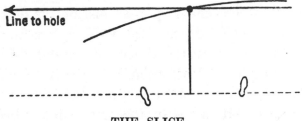

THE SLICE.

The correct stance for an intentional slice is shown, and the track of the club-head across the direct line to the hole.

dropped back an inch and the right moved forward. In this case the hole itself is the direct objective, but the effect of the open stance and of a quick lifting of the club-head in the backward swing is a stroke made across the line of flight. This can be readily appreciated by reference to the diagram on this page.

For the majority of golfers the pull or hook

is not so easy of accomplishment. It is the reversion of the slice in every point that varies from the straight drive. This time it is the left hand that is well on top of the shaft, pushing the right hand round till it faces the ground behind.

Both feet stand squarely on a line parallel with that between ball and hole, with the result that the stance is turned slightly away, just as in slicing it faces more towards the hole. This position of the feet means that the club-head must cut across the direct line earlier in its downward swing than it would do normally. At the moment of impact the weight of the body is held back on the right foot and the right wrist is turned over, as it were, on the ball. This brings the face of the club inwards so that it strikes at an angle, in the same way as the slice follows the outward turning of the face. The result of the inward turning for a pull is termed a " shut face."

It is a good deal harder to hit the ball truly early in the swing than it is to strike it at the last possible moment, and the slightest error in turning or wrist work has more serious consequences. Perhaps the chief mistake to be avoided in practising the pull is a tendency to roll the wrists over too soon. If the face is turned inwards before impact there will be far more overhang than is necessary for giving top-spin, and the ball will be driven into the ground if it be hit at all.

I would repeat that, however fascinating may be such perfect command of the ball that it can be pulled or sliced to a nicety, nevertheless the golfing career of any player is doomed if he undertake these divergences and excursions into the higher finesse of the game before he has entirely mastered the swing and the straight drive.

CHAPTER XV

HOW TO CHEAT THE WIND

SOME years ago I was fortunate in being attached to a seaside club where the wind blew strongly almost every day. I spent many hours of practice and hard work in learning how best to cheat the wind. Under no other conditions is so much skill demanded to keep the ball always under control, but the additional difficulties can be overcome by intelligent practice.

Whether the wind blows across or straight against the tee, the first precaution against its effect is steadiness. If the feet are set a little further apart than usual it will be found easier to stand squarely and firmly upon them. Some loss of driving power may accompany the wide stance, but it will be more than compensated by increased control of club and ball. In the same way a tighter grip must be taken, for a strong wind will sadly upset the swing of a loosely held club.

Practice will soon show how far these modifications of the regular rules are to be carried. A firm stance does not mean stiff, cramped action, nor does a tight grip call for woodenness in the wrists. The degree of restraint must be judged by the individual according to the force and direction of the wind. All that is asked is that balance should be ensured under adverse conditions.

It will be remembered that the position of the ball for an ordinary drive is almost exactly opposite the left heel. When contending with strong wind this position is moved to a point opposite the centre of a line between the feet, so that the ball is equidistant from both. The back swing should be shorter and flatter than usual, in order to avoid offering resistance to the wind. Especially when fighting a head wind it will be found useless to take a full swing back; the shorter, lower swing does not necessitate so much lifting of the left heel and consequently balance is more easily maintained.

When attempting to shorten the swing there is a tendency to cramp the turn of the shoulders. This must be carefully guarded against and the pivoting must be as free and full as for any shot. The shortening of the swing is effected by curtailing the wrist action at the top, not by any decrease in the turn of the upper part of the body. An incomplete pivot results in the shoulders coming round to the ball before the club-head, drawing it across the line of flight and committing a bad slice.

Another mistake easy to make in playing a drive of this sort is that of lurching after the ball, with the idea of keeping it down. A moment's thought will show that such a swaying forward of the body cuts across all the canons of the game ; its outcome is invariably a complete smother. The ball is simply hit in accordance with the instructions given in the chapter on the Drive, except that there is a shorter, straighter swing back and a lower follow-through.

Since the ball has been moved nearer the right foot it follows that the club-head will meet it earlier in the swing, before the furthest point of the arc has been reached. But the impact is only a fraction sooner than usual, if it is too early a slice will be the result. The object of striking before the swing is fully extended is to avoid getting under the ball and lofting it into the wind. The club-head is still on its downward journey when it hits the ball, sending it away with low flight.

When playing in a cross-wind it is necessary to allow for drift. I have found it better to allow for the wind and let it carry the ball, rather than drive the ball straight with pull or slice to hold its own. If the wind is blowing from left to right, play always to the left, imagining the edge of the rough on that side to be the middle of the fairway. Greater length will be obtained in this way than if a pull had been played against the wind. The effect of a cross-wind is always exaggerated in the mind of an inexperienced player. It does its worst with a ball that is spinning through being inaccurately driven. Provided that the hit has been perfectly clean and true, directly at some chosen spot, none but the most tempestuous cross-winds will take it far out of its course.

Whether playing with or against a cross-wind it is folly to attempt to get as much length as under calmer conditions. The natural impulse is to hit harder to counteract the wind's influence, instead of which this is increased. The slogger in wind always beats himself. It must be acknowledged that the wind can and does shorten a drive, and it is useless to try to prove otherwise. Never over-estimate the terrors of a cross- or head-wind, and never under-estimate the importance of steadiness and restraint.

There is always a danger of beating the ground with the sole of the club when hitting the ball before the club-head has reached the bottom of the downward swing. If this happens frequently, it may be corrected by standing back a trifle further from the ball and by teeing somewhat higher. To drive a low ball from a high tee demands great precision of play, and it is not a stroke to be attempted without some practice. The greatest bugbear of those who attempt to play in the wind according to these instructions will be the slice. But this need never occur if the head is kept still, the shoulders properly turned and not swayed, the follow-through low but unrestrained, and the ball struck before— but only just before—the bottom of the swing.

CHAPTER XVI

THE RUN-UP SHOT

In the chapter on the Mashie I touched on two types of approach shot, the run-up and the pitch; their importance entitles them to separate and fuller consideration, so I propose to deal with each in rather more detail, paying particular attention to the necessary modifications in stance.

First, let me dispel the idea that a run-up shot is merely one played from just off the green : the term can be applied equally well to a shot sixty yards from the flag, provided that the ball flies low, and runs. I have always thought of this as a typically Scottish shot, for across the border it is played much more often and, I may add, much better than in England. The reason is to be found in the undulating greens which are a feature of so many courses in Scotland. A pitch shot, played high in the air and dropping almost dead, runs considerable risk of falling on an adverse slope and kicking in the wrong direction ; only a man who could drop his ball on a sixpence can use the pitch with any certainty at all on a great many greens. With some practice and a knowledge of the ground it is safer to rely on the run-up shot. All who know St. Andrews will, I think, readily agree that the run-up pays much better on those bumpy greens.

It is surprising to the inexperienced how truly the ball will keep the line when struck firmly to the hole with this stroke. I am sure that if players on the inland courses of England were to cultivate the run-up shot and use it more often they would be less erratic in their short game and greatly improve their golf generally. I very seldom pitch a ball when it is possible to run up or to use the pitch-and-run shot. This latter is not a compromise, being rather a development of the run-up than any relation to the pitch : it consists in pitching the ball so far and making it run the rest, and its value is found when approaching from forty to sixty yards with no intervening hazards.

Those who have not advanced very far in

the game are well advised to begin with the short run-up before attempting the longer and less easy pitch-and-run. Thorough experience in short distance approach work gives one a sense of the degree of strength to be put into the stroke under different circumstances, as

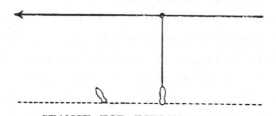

STANCE FOR RUN-UP SHOT.
The feet are close and the right toe points squarely at the ball.

well as the feel of the club and touch of the ball.

I have found a Jigger best adapted to this short running shot, being an iron club with no great amount of loft to its face. The feet should be comparatively close together with the right toe opposite the ball. The forward stance naturally cancels the rule of keeping the shaft at right angles, for the hands inevitably come in front of the club-head.

The club-head is barely lifted from the

ground, nor is it taken far back ; if accurately timed, the shot will carry a surprising distance for so short a swing. Just before impact, by a slight but sharp movement of the right wrist, the face of the club is turned in on the ball to effect a low flight and sufficient top spin to make the ball run.

Such a shot can be played with safety up to a distance of sixty yards, given sufficient skill and absence of obstacles, but in every case it is imperative that the line to the hole should be carefully studied and irregularities of fall and rise allowed for. In playing shots of different lengths it must be remembered that increased carrying power comes not with any forcing action but solely by means of a longer swing. The difficult part of the swing is the timing of the right wrist movement, a foozle of the worst order arising if the face of the club turns in too early or too late. It is well to centre the attention on the club-head rather than on the wrists, leaving them to turn unconsciously.

The pitch-and-run is brought about in much the same way, but it is best played with the Mashie. A somewhat wider stance is taken, though the ball is still played off the right foot. Again, it is important to keep the club-head close to the ground going back and to introduce the same turn of the wrist at the critical moment. This is essentially a wristy shot and consequently one that must be practised a great deal before it can be used with much success. It is the same mechanically as the run-up, with the difference that arises from using a club with greater lofting ability.

Many times I have seen golfers playing for a pitch-and-run and turning their shoulders squarely to the hole early in the follow-through, and so pulling the club round to the left and losing all sense of direction. This is to some an instinctive tendency when lifting the ball under any circumstances; it can only be counteracted by fixing the determination to follow through directly down the line of flight. It is inadvisable to raise the heels at all; the more reason, therefore, for free and smooth knee action. Most important of all is the necessity of being well over the ball and avoiding any suspicion of chop in the stroke.

CHAPTER XVII

PITCHING

ALTHOUGH for most approaches I advise the run-up when the way is clear, or the pitch-and-run when a bunker has to be negotiated some distance from the green, there are occasions upon which it is more advisable to play a high ball that will drop practically dead. It may be that you lie close behind a bunker on the very edge of the green, or perhaps you have to land the ball on a raised green, where any run after landing would be fatal. In these and similar circumstances the pitch shot must be employed.

Without waxing scientific or mathematical it is worth pointing out that the effects of pitching are produced by playing the ball with back spin; this causes it to fly higher than is normally the case and to check its progress upon coming to earth. Back spin is imparted by hitting the ball a downward blow at the back and below with a club that has considerable loft to its face. The Mashie, Mashie Niblick and Niblick are all clubs that may be used according to length demanded, always with the idea of separating the ball from the ground by getting beneath it.

The average player finds difficulty in making the ball rise sufficiently to drop so straight that its run is practically negligible. In attempting to remedy matters he sometimes adopts one of two courses; either he ducks with the shoulders and dislodges a quantity of turf before ever the club-head reaches the ball, or he indulges in an appalling scoop, lifting the club-head abruptly at the moment of impact in the hope of pushing the ball skywards.

It is first of all necessary to dispel any idea that the club cannot do the lofting without well-meant but futile assistance in the nature of scooping. Among the ten clubs I advocate there is at least one that will lift the ball high enough for any emergency. No pitch shot can be played with skill or success until there is a confident belief in the lofting power of correctly applied back spin.

The faster the green, the higher the ball should fly in order that it shall be well under control when it strikes the ground. The art of adjusting this flight lies principally in an intelligent placing of the feet : a correct stance for the business in hand is here, as always, half the battle. For longer pitch shots the heels should be about nine inches apart, with the ball opposite the centre of a

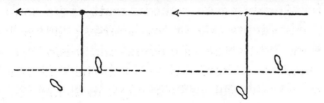

STANCES FOR PITCHING.
The left-hand diagram shows the stance for longer pitch shots, that on the right for short distances.

line between them ; no measurement, however, can serve as anything more than a rough indication of the position that is best judged by a feeling of comfort and security. The left toe is turned towards the hole and the right towards the ball, so bringing the shoulders round to face in front of the ball. The elbows are kept close to the side by means of a stance close up to the ball and a

very upright swing—both essential to good
pitching. The actual hitting does not differ
from other strokes ; it must be remembered
when making the shot that the ball is lofted
by the club-face and not by any contortions
of the body or the wrists. The follow-through
must be properly completed before the club
comes up over the left shoulder, otherwise it
is most difficult to avoid the tendency to
scoop.

The stance for short pitching is more open
than for the longer shots, the ball lying
opposite the left heel. In both cases the face
of the club must be open, or turned back to
face somewhat away from the player, and the
more open the stance the more open should
the club-face be. Back swing and follow-
through are modified according to the length
of shot being played.

Perhaps the most necessary advice I can
give on pitching is that the strokes must be
played firmly and with decision. To create
back spin it follows that more power must be
put into the shot than is usual for the distance
to be covered, and for this reason the pitching
of many players is a half-hearted affair. Do

not be afraid of over-running the hole with
these shots, play them boldly for the flag.
In fact, I have often found it pay to play for
a spot past the hole : the ball rarely carries
too far if correctly played but is sent away
with so much back spin that its run is only a
matter of inches. J. H. Taylor is a great
exponent of the art of laying **a** ball dead ; no
one who watches him can mistake the firmness and neatness with which he plays his
high approaches. Such courage to play one's
pitch shots boldly comes only from confidence,
and that in turn is a product of practice.

CHAPTER XVIII

GOLF WISDOM

In this chapter I want to help, if possible, the many golfers who have not, or who believe they have not, the temperament for golf.

I know of no other game that calls for greater restraint of the feelings. It is not without good reason that the " cussedness " of golf has become a byword, as well as a source of income to innumerable humorists and illustrators. There are so many petty annoyances and little worries that can crop up in the course of a round to put a player off his game, and they are bound to be the source of increasing irritation unless taken in the right spirit. So it is that golf may show up a man's character at its best or at its worst, in accordance with the degree of patience he displays under sore trials. It would not be possible to enumerate here all the distractions which a golfer can suffer, much less to prescribe remedies or preventions, but I hope to reduce the weight of a few of the more common burdens.

Quite the most cheerful and good-humoured fellow will become sullen, nervous and unapproachable when he is playing in a competition. The feeling that he is on trial upsets his usually well-balanced good nature, and the slightest sign of ill-fortune is disastrous to his peace of mind. When a man blames his partner after the pair have lost their match he is generally attempting to excuse himself. Such a one deserves to be despised, but there is a grain of truth in his complaint.

When two players are going round together, either as partners or opponents, they are bound to influence each other's form to some degree, the more highly strung of the two being naturally the more susceptible to the effects of the other's play. There is no doubt whatever that if the mind is allowed to dwell upon the slowness or the speed of a partner's swing there is bound to be a reaction in one's own case. The match player, keyed up to high pitch of nervous tension, is most liable to be affected in this way. Under such circumstances it is safest to avoid all danger of infection and to ignore the other man completely. When drawn to play with a stranger who is noted for particularly quick or slow action, I take good care not to see him play his first few shots. It is a good plan. Look somewhere else, and take no notice of the other ball, you are not able to turn it into a bunker or guide it into safety by following it with your eyes. If you are busy yourself with your own game and keep your opponent's swing right out of your mind for three or four holes, he should trouble you no further however often and however closely you may watch him; the dangerous period is the earliest stage of a round, before you have safely got the feel of your own swing.

In the same way bad play will quickly make itself felt upon a partner or an opponent. There is always the temptation to take less trouble when playing with a poor golfer or one much below form, but if this slackness is indulged it is not long before there are two men off their game instead of one. One of the curiosities of golf matches is the number of people who are ready to sink at once to the level of their partner; obviously the worse one's partner plays the harder should one try to restore the balance by doing well, yet how few put such simple common sense into practice.

So many passably good golfers have been painfully surprised in medal competitions, for instance, that only the hopelessly foolish should be guilty of under-estimating an opponent's possibilities. A player who has attained the dignity of a single-figure handicap is drawn against one who is still struggling in the twenties ; the short handicap man sees little need to exert himself, allows his game to get slack, and discovers too late that he cannot save the match. I have made it a rule never to play slackly, whoever my opponent may be. I play every shot to the best of my ability. It is a matter of courtesy as well as of sound tactics never to lower one's standard to that of another.

Many holes have been lost by indifferently played approach shots. An advantage of two up before getting on the green may seem to justify the certainty of winning the hole easily enough, but it is by no means a sufficient reason for playing a careless Mashie shot with the object of landing somewhere on the green rather than as near as possible to the hole. I have seen such a player considerably taken aback by his opponent holing out with a chip shot and taking the hole, while it commonly happens under such circumstances that the man who is down will sink a long putt and halve the hole. Every shot must be played for the flag : if the other lays his approach dead you naturally try to do the same, but if he takes two or three in getting within putting distance you should still aim as grimly to be close to the hole in one.

The unexpected loss of a hole, whether in the manner I have described or in any other way, has a far-reaching effect on the whole game. A player's calmness and temper are disturbed by losing a point that he knows he should have won, and it is difficult to make up again the smallest loss of self-confidence. Like any other vice, slackness in golf is far easier to acquire than to be rid of ; if good luck sends you a poor opponent do not abuse your fortune, but play your best throughout, improve your game, and incidentally make sure of the match.

Everyone, even the non-golfer, knows the man who is put off his shot by the slightest movement or sound. Nobody denies that it does not help to be surrounded with distractions when playing the ball, but this is no reason for such extreme sensitiveness as is displayed by so many. The patron saint of these irritable individuals is a cantankerous colonel advancing, purple-faced and murderous, upon an unfortunate caddy who has dared to lift an eyelid. There is, too often, very little exaggeration in such a picture.

A friend of mine became exceedingly irate should anyone stand behind him or move a club when he was putting but, being a doctor, he determined to find a cure for his complaint. His plan was simple. One morning he arrived at the first tee and told an astonished caddy that he would be given sixpence every time he put him off, provided of course that he behaved no less reasonably than usual. Fortunately the caddy was of rare honesty and, by exercising the greatest restraint and concentration on his game, my friend was only a shilling or two out of pocket at the end of the round. In this way he soon learnt to give all his attention to his stroke.

Temperamental failings, as just shown, can be conquered. The weakness of becoming irritated by any trifling distraction rapidly grows worse, unless taken firmly in hand, and may reach the stage in which the mere expectation of some movement or noise ruins the sufferer's play even when nothing whatever actually occurs to take his attention from the ball.

Not a few golfers are upset by playing against longer hitters than themselves. Do not worry about the man who persistently outdrives you ; concentrate entirely on your own game, play your natural swing, and strive all the time to keep straight. His gain of a few yards on the drive is very far from meaning that he will win the hole, he will usually find the bunkers as great an obstacle as you do yourself. You will have an advantage in playing the second shot before he does, and you must play it with the conviction that if it is a really good one you will disturb your opponent and make his task a great deal harder. The player who by nature is restricted to the short game must make himself accurate above everything else, only thus can he balance his deficiency in long shots and make up on the green what he may lose on the fairway.

There are pitfalls, too, for the long hitter. He is apt to believe that all opponents can be beaten by being outdriven from every tee. If this idea is at the back of one's mind it leads to pressing the longer shots and finding rough grass and hazards placed by nature and the architect for the unwary. The man who is obsessed with the desire to get length above everything most often beats himself, and ability to control hitting power stands alone between what may be an asset or a handicap.

If a golfer is hasty and headstrong it will pay him far more to cultivate a little deliberation and restraint than to develop his Iron play, for example. I have not forgotten the proverbs of faint heart and nothing venture, but in golf it is better for one's style and in no way less exciting or interesting to play for safety. When you are in doubt about your chances of carrying a bunker play a shot

short and try to find the hole with a second.
Nine times out of ten the straining to carry
beyond an obstacle will drop the ball into it,
whereas there is infinitely more golf in playing
discreetly up to the hazard and then approaching skilfully over it.   There is the confidence
born of certainty in using clubs for work well
within their power, and this in itself will
increase the quality of your play.   In the
same way, when playing from rough grass or
out of a bunker, it is foolish to take a Mashie
unless you know you can get the ball up
with it—use a Mashie Niblick instead, and
you will suffer no loss in length.

In dealing with medal and competition
play I have referred to only some of the
distractions that may arise or be imagined.
But there are other features of this type of
game that deserve consideration.   Most important of all is complete concentration on
your own game, every shot played with the
care and determination given to a final putt,
and no undue notice taken of other people's
doings.   There are, nevertheless, dangers
attending such engrossment : a man who is
entirely wrapped up in his own play must be

prepared to treat misfortunes philosophically, to take quietly what luck comes his way, and to exaggerate neither his successes nor his failures. Those who are blessed or cursed with vivid imaginations must keep them strictly in hand, otherwise they will think they see the bunkers on the right swallow up the ball, or imagine they hear a splash in the pond to the left—and surely enough a slice or a pull will be the outcome. If all the powers of mind and body are utilised with the object of getting to the flag there will be no room for gloomy contemplation. This advice is properly only for the so-called temperamental players, but it applies to everyone to some extent.

At Wanstead there is a lake that must be carried from the tee. It has been claimed as the most expensive hole in the world, and with some reason, for several hundreds of balls find a watery grave there each year. I have been round this particular course time and again with men who have played the twelve holes preceding the lake with perfect confidence, driving down the fairway every time straight enough and far enough to carry the lake with ease. They arrive at the thirteenth and promptly drop their drives into the water. This is being done every week by players who are the last to be thought temperamental or unnecessarily affected by nerves and imagination : it is a proof that all of us are liable to be influenced, however unconsciously, by what we are afraid we may or may not do. In this particular instance I have watched especially carefully and noticed that the swing is rarely so free and confident as in the previous drives. If there was the conviction that the lake was going to be carried, it would be done.

So, too, with bunkers at the side of the fairway. It would be an interesting experiment to make a hole with movable bunkers alongside ; I have no doubt whatever that 50 per cent. more players would keep straight down the middle when the bunkers were absent than when the same men played with them in position. The fear of the consequences of a mistake so often lead to that very mistake being made that one is tempted to prescribe a course of mind-discipline or cultivation of will-power for aspiring golfers.

The only remedy I can suggest here is concentration on playing the particular shot correctly to the exclusion of all else.

Most cyclists and motorists of experience have known the danger of steering unconsciously towards some object which has for the moment attracted all their attention. The same is true in golf, the beginner is less likely to be led astray than one who has passed the stage when he had to concentrate absolutely on his play to get any result whatever. There comes a time when the attention may wander just a little, and still a passable shot be played, never a good one; it is then that a stranger on the course just within range will inevitably attract the ball of a player who has allowed his mind to be concerned, however little, with the possibility of hitting him. The moral is not far to seek; if the middle of the fairway or the flag is on one's mind, what should be the result?

I will take the liberty of giving a personal example of the value of being wrapped up in one's own game. At a Mid-Surrey tournament in 1920 I played against Abe Mitchell. It was the first time I had been pitted against so great a golfer, and I was only an assistant at the time ; a few days previously, however, I had won the Welsh Championship, and so was at the top of my form. The first two rounds of this tournament gave me little trouble, but when I found myself up against Abe, who at that time was carrying all before him, I must confess to misgivings. Following my rule, I determined to play my best game by putting into it everything I knew, so having little thought or attention to spare for my opponent.

The first four holes I did in par figures, but I lost three of them. Realising that nothing I could do would have much effect on Mitchell's play, I persevered with my own game and at the eighteenth hole discovered that we were all square. He eventually beat me with a birdie three at the twenty-first. There and then I learnt the lesson of playing my game regardless of anyone else ; sometimes I did not even see where the opposing ball had gone, so concentrated was I on carrying out my own shots correctly.

When watching reputed stylists playing exhibition games or taking part in competitions there is a strong temptation to indulge oneself the whole time in the pleasure of watching the effect rather than the cause of their excellence. Such opportunities ought to be used for serious study. It is not sufficient merely to watch a good player's action, one ought to take the trouble to compare one's own style with his and to discover exactly in which points the difference lies.

There is an art in getting the full benefit from these object lessons in golf. See how a really good player takes his stance ; with his club properly gripped he approaches the ball from behind his final standing position, places his right foot first, and then feels about, as it were, with his left before settling into a correct and comfortable stance. Such details may seem trifling to the uninitiated, but a golfer knows the value of taking pains in the small things.

Almost weekly I see instances of a player being 4 down and 5 to play, and then squaring or winning the match. I remember once how I was 5 up and 6 to play against an 8 handicap man, ready to bet any money that, on his form, he would lose. But he holed two long putts, I went into two bunkers, and we finished all square. All of which goes to show that it is foolish to think a game lost or won before it is finished : the most relentless opponent will sometimes give away chances, and those who know how to take them win.

If you do lose a game, remember its lessons, but forget that you have lost. Concentrate whole-heartedly on your own play, and when within range, aim for the flag and not roughly the middle of the green ; the object in your mind is the hole, not the bunker, and the latter will give little trouble if all your powers are centred in playing to the pin.

CHAPTER XIX

HOW TO PRACTISE

THE majority of people playing golf to-day did not take up the game until they were developed men and women. Many of those who are learning now are past the first flush of youth in which a new game presents comparatively less difficulty than in later years.

A man has, perhaps, been a good footballer, and at thirty or thirty-five begins to find that the game is too strenuous a recreation at the end of a busy week. He is advised to turn to golf. Here he finds friends whose knowledge and ability at football is elementary beside his own, yet they appear to have little difficulty in playing a respectable game of golf. The newcomer puts two and two together, as he thinks, and sees no reason why he should not rapidly overtake his less athletic fellows. Then it is that he will discover that only constant and patient practice can produce good golf, and he will be reminded that it took all the most impressionable years of his life to bring his football to a pitch of excellence. The same truth, of course, applies to the woman who forsakes hockey or another game for golf, and finds that her progress will not bear comparison with her enthusiasm.

I mention these " converts " particularly, because it is almost always such people who are most impatient when they begin the game ; it is easy enough to understand the distaste with which a proficient sportsman in one direction regards his position as a beginner in another. The new player who has never before enjoyed success in any game has no illusion as to the difficulty of his task. To the many who are anxious to step straight on to the links after six or twelve lessons I say here and now that they cannot expect to play round on an equality with friends who have practised the game for years and anticipate a reaching of their standard in a few weeks or even months. Golf is just as difficult as any other game, not a few would say that it is considerably more so, and it demands as much and as frequent practice as possible.

As soon as I could walk with safety I used to borrow balls from my father and clubs from my elder brothers, and spend every evening hitting about in a rough field. As often as not the balls were soon lost, but I would go on swishing at anything and everything I could see—tufts of grass, leaves, match sticks—until I was absolutely tired out. Later on I was allowed to caddy at the local links, and so had the chance of watching all manner of styles and peculiarities of swinging the club ; these were imitated in the evening on my patch of rough, with or without a ball, and the result was entertainment as profitable as it was enjoyable. I write this to stress a fact of which I am convinced, that any success I have had or may have in the future is in very large measure due to the countless number of times I have swung the club in perpetual practice from my youth up.

No opportunity of swinging should be missed by young or middle-aged ; every player knows how frequently odd chances occur in the course of a day's golf. I have

sometimes heard expressions of surprise that
a caddy can hit the ball so cleanly when he
gets so few opportunities of actually playing.
There is no mystery in this, for every good
caddy practises the swing until it is part of
his second nature.

A common complaint among week-end
golfers is that they develop a stiffness in the
wrists between one Saturday or Sunday and
another. The remedy is obviously to be
found in a few minutes' wielding of a club
each day ; this will not only strengthen the
wrists and keep them supple, but will also,
if intelligently practised, prove of enormous
benefit in perfecting a good grip.

The same principle applies immediately
before play : do not be in too great a hurry
to get on to the first tee, but give yourself
time for a few preliminary swings. Always
aim at a blade of grass in the same position
as the ball would be, otherwise more harm
than good will come of your practice. Observ-
ance of this advice gives deeper benefit than
just a loosening of the muscles, it prepares
one for the game in the same comprehensive
way as does a knock-up before tennis or a

few balls at the nets before an innings at cricket. Naturally, any swinging or shadow play in practice must be carried out with as scrupulous care as if in play ; there are a great many who know to their cost how easy it is to acquire a careless habit.

When I had the good fortune to be promoted second assistant to the pro. at my local links I determined to model my style on that of one of the great golfers. It was some years before there was an opportunity of seeing any of them, and then the day arrived when I was drawn to play with Harry Vardon in an open competition on another course. This was my chance of picking up knowledge from a past master of the game.

I remember vividly the impression of disappointment at the end of that day's play with Vardon. I seemed to have learned nothing. There was no outstanding feature of his play that thrust itself upon one's notice ; he did everything in such an easy natural way that he appeared to strike the ball with no great effort—and yet it flew away down the fairway much further than my own.

On my way home I reflected that all he

tried to do was to swing his club in the easiest manner possible and carry the ball away in doing so. As soon as I arrived I bolted to the links, took out my driver, and swung exactly as I remembered Vardon doing. Without attempting to hit a ball, I swung the club backwards and forwards at an easy even pace, increasing the speed a little at the bottom of the swing. When I came to put this method into practice I was astonished at the result. My ball was longer without the previous amount of effort, and I realised that I had learnt the secret of timing, a secret that cannot be explained, but is only felt when brain, body and club are working perfectly together.

When going out to practise it is very important to know what the true swing is, and to follow conscientiously the main principles. Plod steadily along instead of getting impatient for good results, remembering that it is better to make a poor effort in the right way than to throw all orthodoxy to the winds for the sake of slight temporary improvement. If the swing has been perfected in practice without a ball it only remains to keep the

mind on the club-head for direction and pace
when actually playing.   There comes a time
when the tiresome hours of practice are found
worth while by a sudden discovery of the
knack of correct timing and hitting.

If any proof were needed of the benefits of
thorough practice it could be found across the
Atlantic.   In 1914 America was behind England in talent, and now she would seem to
have overtaken us.   Such splendid golfers as
Bobby Jones, Hagen, Farrell and Diegel—to
name but a few—have acquired their skill by
constant and thorough practice.   The American treatment of the game is definitely more
scientific than our own, being founded on
hard thinking and painstaking care.   To bear
out this statement I will say that the golf
emigrants, Jim Barnes, Jock Hutchison,
Macdonald and Alex Smith, Tommy Armour,
Bobby Cruickshank and Cyril Walker, would
not have become such great players had they
stayed at home; five of these have won the
highest honours in America.

The British professionals who have crossed
the Atlantic at various times have made
American golf, and American golf has made

them; their employers were not slow to
pick their brains, giving in return the
advantages of training planned with fore-
thought and deliberation. Writers on the
game are often obsessed with the bugbear of
" temperament," pointing to Walter Hagen
as an example of the ideal golf temperament
as against Abe Mitchell. Hagen himself
would be the first to admit Mitchell's great-
ness, and yet the latter cannot win the British
Open Championship. There can be no doubt
that temperament does count: Hagen has
absolute confidence in himself, born of hours
and hours of practice, and any of us who wish
to win the big events must acquire the same
frame of mind in the same way.

The British Isles are well blessed with
courses on which to practise. Scotland pro-
vides all types of golf on courses that vary
in their characteristics so that every shot in
the game presents itself. Any who are able
to take advantage of the links at Gleneagles,
perhaps the finest of inland courses, Troon,
Western Gailes, Prestwick and the like,
should do so with a full sense of their benefits; under such circumstances a player with

average ability can raise himself to the first
class by intelligent practice.   In Wales, too,
there are excellent seaside courses at Porth-
cawl, Southerndown, Pennard, Tenby and
elsewhere—yet few outstanding golfers are
Welsh.   The success of Welsh football under
both codes is largely due to general enthusiasm, and there is no reason why some
interest of a similar kind should not be shown
in golf.   Golfing societies everywhere are
providing valuable opportunities for competi-
tive golf, but if players are to be produced of
a calibre to compete with the Americans
there must be specialised preparation and
thoughtful persistent practice.

CHAPTER XX

ESSENTIALS OF GOOD GOLF

FOR a final chapter I have gathered together the most important of the unwritten rules that should make a good golfer of the average man who keeps them. These do not pretend to be in any way a complete summary of the instructions that precede them, nor will the committing of them to memory ensure inevitable success in competitions and championship play. But I firmly believe that a great deal of good can result by the occasional reading of such maxims, provided they are taken seriously to heart. Let the player who imagines he has done with textbooks read each of these admonitions and ask himself honestly whether he observes them all.

I. Keep your head perfectly steady until the ball has been sent well on its way.

II.   A proper grip is worth the attention
       it deserves.

III.   For all shots keep the elbows down
       and the arms reasonably close to
       the body.   The hands should be as
       far away from the body as possible
       without taking the elbows with
       them.

IV.   Keep your wrists above the shaft
       when addressing the ball, under the
       shaft at the top of the swing and at
       the finish.

V.   With the weight between the feet,
       keep good balance throughout the
       swing.

VI.   When swinging down, force the
       club-head with the wrists and turn
       the shoulders smartly.

VII.   Remember that distance in driving
       depends on the speed which the
       club-head acquires through perfect
       timing of all the movements in the
       swing.

VIII. Make the club-head follow through
       by means of the right arm and right
       shoulder.

IX. Practise often, both with a ball and
without ; do so only when you are
fresh, and treat it with the same care
as actual play.

X. Be patient.

THE RULES OF GOLF

RULES OF THE GAME OF GOLF

APPROVED BY THE ROYAL AND ANCIENT
GOLF CLUB OF ST ANDREWS

REVISED TO DATE

DEFINITIONS

(1) A " side " consists either of one player or of two players. If one player play against another, the match is called " a single." If two play against two, each side playing one ball, the match is called " a foursome." If one play against two, playing one ball between them, the match is called " a three-some."

(2) " Advice " is any counsel or suggestion which could influence a player in determining the line of play, in the choice of a club, or in the method of making a stroke.

(3) The " course " is the whole area within which play is permitted; more particularly, it is the ground between the holes which is specially prepared for play.

(4) The " teeing-ground " is the starting place for a hole. The front of each teeing-ground shall be indicated by two marks placed in a line as nearly as possible at right angles to the line of play, and the

teeing-ground shall include a rectangular space of the depth of two club lengths directly behind the line indicated by the two marks.

(5) " Through the green " is all ground on which play is permitted, except hazards and the putting-green of the hole that is being played.

(6) A " hazard " is any bunker, water (except casual water), ditch (unless excepted by Local Rule), bush, sand, path, or road. Sand blown on to the grass, or sprinkled on the course for its preservation, bare patches, sheep-tracks, snow, and ice are not hazards.

(7) " Casual water " is any temporary accumulation of water (whether caused by rainfall, flooding, or otherwise) which is not one of the ordinary and recognised hazards of the course.

(8) " Out of bounds " is all ground on which play is prohibited.

(9) A ball is " out of bounds " when the greater part of it lies within a prohibited area.

(10) The " putting-green " is all ground, except hazards, within twenty yards of the hole.

(11) The hole shall be $4\frac{1}{4}$ inches in diameter and at least 4 inches deep. If a metal lining be used, it shall be sunk below the lip of the hole and its outer diameter shall not exceed $4\frac{1}{4}$ inches.

(12) The term " loose impediments " denotes any obstructions not fixed or growing, and includes dung, worm-casts, mole-hills, snow and ice.

(13) A " stroke " is the forward movement of the club made with the intention of striking the ball, or any contact between the head of the club and the ball resulting in movement of the ball, except in the

case of a ball accidentally knocked off a tee (Rule 2 (1)).

(14) A " penalty stroke " is a stroke added to the score of a side under certain rules, and does not affect the rotation of play.

(15) The side which plays off first from a teeing-ground is said to have the " honour."

(16) In " teeing," the ball may be placed on the ground, or on sand or other substance in order to raise it off the ground.

(17) A player has " addressed the ball " when he has taken his stance and grounded his club, or, if in a hazard, when he has taken his stance preparatory to striking at the ball.

(18) A ball is " in play " as soon as the player has made a stroke at a teeing-ground, and it remains in play until holed out, except when lifted in accordance with the rules.

(19) A ball is deemed to " move " if it leave its original position in the least degree ; but it is not considered to " move " if it merely oscillate and come to rest in its original position.

(20) A ball is " lost " if it be not found within five minutes after the search for it has begun.

(21) The reckoning of strokes is kept by the terms —" the odd," " two more," " three more," etc., and " one off three," " one off two," " the like." The reckoning of holes is kept by the terms—so many " holes up," or " all even," and so many " to play."

A side is said to be " dormie " when it is as many holes up as there are holes remaining to be played.

(22) An " Umpire " decides questions of fact ; a " Referee " decides questions of Golfing law.

GENERAL AND THROUGH THE GREEN

RULE 1

(1) The Game of Golf is played by two sides, each playing its own ball, with clubs and balls made in conformity with the directions laid down in the clause on " Form and Make of Golf Clubs and Balls."

The game consists in each side playing a ball from a teeing-ground into a hole by successive strokes. The hole is won by the side which holes its ball in fewer strokes than the opposing side, except as otherwise provided for in the Rules.

The hole is halved if both sides hole out in the same number of strokes.

(2) A match consists of one round of the course unless it be otherwise agreed. A match is won by the side which is leading by a number of holes greater than the number of holes remaining to be played.

A match is halved if each side win the same number of holes.

Matches constituted of singles, threesomes, or foursomes shall have precedence of and be entitled to pass any other kind of match.

A single player has no standing, and shall always give way to a match of any kind.

Any match playing a whole round shall be entitled to pass a match playing a shorter round.

If a match fail to keep its place on the green, and lose in distance more than one clear hole on the players in front, it may be passed, on request being made.

Rule 2

(1) A match begins by each side playing a ball from the first teeing-ground.

A ball played from outside the limits of the teeing-ground may be at once recalled by the opposing side, and may be re-teed without penalty.

If a ball, when not in play, fall off a tee, or be knocked off a tee by the player in addressing it, it may be re-teed without penalty; if the ball be struck when so moving, no penalty shall be incurred.

(2) The option of taking the honour at the first teeing-ground shall, if necessary, be decided by lot.

A ball played by a player when his opponent should have had the honour may be at once recalled by the opposing side, and may be re-teed without penalty.

The side which wins a hole shall take the honour at the next teeing-ground. If a hole has been halved, the side which had the honour at the previous teeing-ground shall retain it.

On beginning a new match, the winner of the long match in the previous round shall take the honour; if the previous long match was halved, the side which last won a hole shall take the honour.

Rule 3

In a threesome or foursome the partners shall strike off alternately from the teeing-grounds, and shall strike alternately during the play of each hole.

If a player play when his partner should have played, his side shall lose the hole.

RULE 4

(1) A player may not ask for nor willingly receive advice from anyone except his own caddie, his partner, or his partner's caddie.

(2) A player is entitled at any time during the play of a hole to ascertain from his opponent the number of strokes the latter has played; if the opponent give wrong information as to the number of strokes he has played, he shall lose the hole, unless he correct his mistake before the player has played another stroke.

(3) A player may employ a fore-caddie, but may not receive advice from him.

(4) When playing through the green, or from a hazard, a player may have the line to the hole indicated to him, but no mark shall be placed nor shall anyone stand on the proposed line, in order to indicate it, while the stroke is being made.

The penalty for a breach of this Rule shall be the loss of the hole.

RULE 5

The ball must be fairly struck at with the head of the club, not pushed, scraped, nor spooned.

The penalty for a breach of this Rule shall be the loss of the hole.

RULE 6

A ball must be played wherever it lies or the hole be given up, except as otherwise provided for in the Rules and Local Rules.

Note.—For a lost or unplayable ball see Rule 22 ; for a ball out of bounds see Rule 23.

RULE 7

When the balls are in play, the ball farther from the hole shall be played first. Through the green, or in a hazard, if a player play when his opponent should have played, the opponent may at once recall the stroke. A ball so recalled shall be dropped as near as possible to the place where it lay, without penalty.

For teeing-ground, see Rule 2 (2) ; for putting-green, see Rule 31 (2).

RULE 8

A ball shall be dropped in the following manner : —The player himself shall drop it. He shall face the hole, stand erect, and drop the ball behind him over his shoulder.

The penalty for a breach of this Rule shall be the loss of the hole.

If, in the act of dropping, the ball touch the player, he shall incur no penalty, and, if it roll into a hazard, the player may redrop the ball without penalty.

RULE 9

(1) A ball in play may not be touched before the hole is played out, except as provided for in the Rules.

The penalty for a breach of this Rule shall be one stroke.

The player may, without penalty, touch his ball with his club in the act of addressing it, provided he does not move the ball.

A ball in play may with the opponent's consent

be lifted for the purpose of identification, but it must be carefully replaced.

(2) If the player's ball move the opponent's ball through the green or in a hazard, the opponent, if he choose, may drop a ball, without penalty, as near as possible to the place where his ball lay, but this must be done before another stroke is played by either side.

RULE 10

In playing through the green, irregularities of surface which could in any way affect the player's stroke shall not be removed nor pressed down by the player, his partner, or either of their caddies ; a player is, however, always entitled to place his feet firmly on the ground when taking his stance.

The penalty for a breach of this Rule shall be the loss of the hole.

RULE 11

Any flag-stick, guide-flag, movable guide-post, wheelbarrow, tool, roller, grass-cutter, box, vehicle, or similar obstruction may be removed. A ball moved in removing such an obstruction shall be replaced without penalty. A ball lying on or touching such an obstruction, or lying on or touching clothes, or nets, or ground under repair or covered up or opened for the purpose of the upkeep of the course, or lying in one of the holes, or in a guide-flag hole, or in a hole made by the greenkeeper, may be lifted and dropped without penalty as near as possible to the place where it lay, but not nearer to the hole. A ball lifted in a hazard, under such circumstances, shall be dropped in the hazard.

RULE 12

(1) Any loose impediment lying within a club length of the ball and not being in or touching a hazard, may be removed without penalty; if the ball move after any such loose impediment has been touched by the player, his partner, or either of their caddies, the player shall be deemed to have caused the ball to move, and the penalty shall be one stroke.

(2) A loose impediment lying more than a club length from the ball may not be moved under penalty of the loss of the hole, unless the loose impediment lie on the putting-green (see Rule 28 (1)).

(3) When a ball is in play, if a player or his partner, or either of their caddies accidentally move his or their ball, or by touching anything cause it to move, the penalty shall be one stroke.

(4) If a ball in play move after the player has grounded his club in the act of addressing it, or, if a ball in play being in a hazard move after the player has taken his stance to play it, he shall be deemed to have caused it to move, and the penalty shall be one stroke.

NOTE.—If the player has lifted a loose impediment (see Rules 12 (1) and 28 (1)), and the ball has not moved until the player has grounded his club, he shall only be deemed to have caused the ball to move under Section (4) of this Rule, and the penalty shall be one stroke.

RULE 13

A player shall not play while his ball is moving, under the penalty of the loss of the hole, except in

the case of a teed ball (Rule 2), or a ball struck twice
(Rule 14), or a ball in water (Rule 26). When the
ball only begins to move while the player is making
his backward or forward swing, he shall incur no
penalty under this Rule, but he is not exempted from
the provisions of Rule 12 (1) or Rule 28 (1) and of
Rule 12 (3) and (4).

Rule 14

If a player, when making a stroke, strike the ball
twice, the penalty shall be one stroke, but he shall
incur no further penalty by reason of his having
played while his ball was moving.

Rule 15

Before striking at a ball in play, a player shall not
move, bend, nor break anything fixed or growing,
except so far as is necessary to enable him fairly to
take his stance in addressing the ball, or in making
his backward or forward swing. The club may only
be grounded lightly, and not pressed on the ground.

The penalty for a breach of this Rule shall be the
loss of the hole.

Rule 16

When the balls lie within a club length of each
other through the green or in a hazard, the ball lying
nearer to the hole may, at the option of either the
player or the opponent, be lifted until the other ball
is played, and shall then be replaced as near as
possible to the place where it lay.

If either ball be accidentally moved in complying

with this Rule, no penalty shall be incurred, and the ball so moved shall be replaced.

If the lie of the lifted ball be altered in playing the other ball, the lifted ball may be placed as near as possible to the place where it lay and in a lie similar to that which it originally occupied.

RULE 17

(1) If a ball *in motion* be stopped or deflected by any agency outside the match, or by a fore-caddie, it is a rub of the green and the ball shall be played from the spot where it lies.

(2) If a ball lodge in *anything moving*, a ball shall be dropped, or if on the putting-green, placed, as near as possible to the place where the object was when the ball lodged in it, without penalty.

(3) If a ball *at rest* be displaced by any agency outside the match, except wind, the player shall drop a ball as near as possible to the place where it lay, without penalty; and if the ball be displaced on the putting-green, it shall be replaced without penalty.

RULE 18

If a player's ball when *in motion* be interfered with in any way by an opponent or his caddie, or his clubs, the opponent's side shall lose the hole.

If a player's ball when *at rest* be moved by an opponent or his caddie, or his clubs, the opponent's side shall lose the hole, except as provided for in Rules 9 (2), 16, 21 (3), 31 (1), 32 (2), and 33.

Rule 19

If a player's ball strike or be stopped by himself, or his partner, or either of their caddies, or their clubs, his side shall lose the hole.

Rule 20

(1) If a player play the opponent's ball his side shall lose the hole, unless :—

(*a*) The opponent then play the player's ball, in which case the penalty is cancelled, and the hole shall be played out with the balls thus exchanged.

(*b*) The mistake occur through wrong information given by an opponent or his caddie, in which case there shall be no penalty ; if the mistake be discovered before the opponent has played, it shall be rectified by dropping a ball as near as possible to the place where the opponent's ball lay.

On the putting-green the ball shall be replaced.

(2) If a player play a stroke with the ball of anyone not engaged in the match, and the mistake be discovered and intimated to his opponent before his opponent has played his next stroke, there shall be no penalty ; if the mistake be not discovered and so intimated until after the opponent has played his next stroke, the player's side shall lose the hole.

Rule 21

(1) If a ball lie in fog, bent, bushes, long grass, or the like, only so much thereof shall be touched as will enable the player to find his ball.

(2) If a ball be completely covered by sand, only so much thereof may be removed as will enable the

player to see the top of the ball ; if the ball be touched in removing the sand, no penalty shall be incurred.

(3) If a player or his caddie when searching for an opponent's ball accidentally touch or move it, no penalty shall be incurred, and the ball, if moved, shall be replaced.

The penalty for a breach of this Rule shall be the loss of the hole.

RULE 22

(1) If a ball be lost (except in water or casual water) or be deemed by the player to be unplayable, the player shall play his next stroke as nearly as possible at the spot from which the ball which is lost or unplayable was played, adding a penalty stroke to the score for the hole.

If the stroke was played from the teeing-ground, a ball may be teed ; in all other cases a ball shall be dropped.

(2) In order to save delay, if a ball has been played on to a part of the course where it is likely to be lost or unplayable, the player may at once play another ball in the manner provided for in this Rule, but if the first ball be neither lost nor unplayable it shall continue in play without penalty.

RULE 23

(1) If a ball lie out of bounds, the player shall play his next stroke as nearly as possible at the spot from which the ball which is out of bounds was played, adding a penalty stroke to the score for the hole.

If the stroke was played from the teeing-ground

a ball may be teed ; in all other cases a ball shall be dropped.

In the case of a ball played out of bounds, the penalty stroke may be remitted by Local Rule (see Note).

(2) In order to save delay, if a player, after making a stroke considers that his ball may be out of bounds, he may at once play another ball in the manner provided for in this Rule, but if it be discovered that his first ball is not out of bounds, it shall continue in play without penalty.

NOTE.—*Out of Bounds*.—If the penalty stroke has been remitted by Local Rule and a provisional ball has been played under these conditions, on reaching the place where the first ball is likely to be, if the player or his opponent be still in doubt, the player is not entitled to presume that the first ball is out of bounds till he has made a search of five minutes.

(3) A player has the right at any time of ascertaining whether his opponent's ball is out of bounds or not, before his opponent can compel him to continue his play.

(4) A player may stand out of bounds to play a ball lying within bounds.

RULE 24

If a ball split into separate pieces, another ball may be dropped where any piece lies. If a ball crack or become unfit for play, the player may change it on intimating to his opponent his intention to do so. Mud adhering to a ball shall not be considered as making it unfit for play.

HAZARDS AND CASUAL WATER

RULE 25

When a ball lies in or touches a hazard, nothing shall be done which can in any way improve its lie : the club shall not touch the ground, nor shall anything be touched, or moved, before the player strikes at the ball, subject to the following exceptions : (1) The player may place his feet firmly on the ground for the purpose of taking his stance ; (2) in addressing the ball, or in the backward or forward swing, any grass, bent, bush, or other growing substance, or the side of a bunker, wall, paling, or other immovable obstacle may be touched ; (3) steps or planks placed in a hazard by the Green Committee for access to or egress from such hazard, or any obstruction mentioned in Rule 11, may be removed, and if a ball be moved in so doing, it shall be replaced without penalty ; (4) any loose impediment may be lifted from the putting-green ; (5) the player shall be entitled to find his ball as provided for by Rule 21.

The penalty for a breach of this Rule shall be the loss of the hole.

RULE 26

When a ball is in water a player may, without penalty, strike at it while it is moving, but he must not delay to make his stroke in order to allow the wind or current to better the position of the ball, under penalty of the loss of the hole.

Rule 27

(1) If a ball lie or be lost in a recognised water hazard (whether the ball lie in water or not) the player may drop a ball under penalty of one stroke either (*a*) behind the hazard, keeping the spot at which the ball crossed the margin of the hazard between himself and the hole, or (*b*) in the hazard, keeping the spot at which the ball entered the water between himself and the hole.

(2) If a ball lie or be lost in casual water through the green, the player may drop a ball, without penalty, within two club lengths of the margin, as near as possible to the spot where the ball lay, but not nearer to the hole.

If a ball when dropped roll into the water it may be re-dropped without penalty.

(3) If a ball on the putting-green lie in casual water, or if casual water intervene between a ball lying on the putting-green and the hole, the ball may be played where it lies, or it may be lifted without penalty and placed by hand, either within two club lengths directly behind the spot from which the ball was lifted, or in the nearest position to that spot which is not nearer to the hole, and which affords a putt to the hole without casual water intervening.

(4) A ball lying so near to casual water that the water interferes with the player's stance may be treated as if it lay in casual water, under the preceding Sections of this Rule.

(5) If it be impossible from want of space in which to play, or from any other cause, for a player to drop a ball in conformity with Sections (1) and (2)

of this Rule, or to place it in conformity with Section (3), he shall " drop " or " place " as nearly as possible within the limits laid down in these Sections but not nearer to the hole.

The penalty for a breach of this Rule shall be the loss of the hole.

PUTTING-GREEN

Rule 28

(1) Any loose impediment may be lifted from the putting-green, irrespective of the position of the player's ball. If the player's ball, when on the putting-green, move after any loose impediment lying within six inches of it has been touched by the player, his partner, or either of their caddies, the player shall be deemed to have caused it to move, and the penalty shall be one stroke.

(2) Dung, wormcasts, snow, and ice may be scraped aside with a club, but the club must not be laid with more than its own weight upon the ground nor must anything be pressed down either with the club or in any other way.

(3) The line of the putt must not be touched, except by placing the club immediately in front of the ball in the act of addressing it, and as above authorised.

The penalty for a breach of this Rule shall be the loss of the hole.

Rule 29

(1) When the player's ball is on the putting-green, the player's caddie, his partner, or his partner's caddie may, before the stroke is played, point out a

direction for putting, but in doing this they shall not touch the ground on the proposed line of putt. No mark shall be placed anywhere on the putting-green.

(2) Any player or caddie engaged in the match may stand at the hole, but no player or caddie shall endeavour, by moving or otherwise, to influence the action of the wind upon the ball.

A player is, however, always entitled to send his own caddie to stand at the hole while he plays his stroke.

Either side may refuse to allow a person who is not engaged in the match to stand at the hole.

The penalty for a breach of this Rule shall be the loss of the hole.

RULE 30

When the player's ball lies on the putting-green, he shall not play until the opponent's ball is at rest.

The penalty for a breach of this Rule shall be the loss of the hole.

RULE 31

(1) When the balls lie within six inches of each other on the putting-green (the distance to be measured from their nearest points), the ball lying nearer to the hole may, at the option of either the player or the opponent, be lifted until the other ball is played, and the lifted ball shall then be replaced as near as possible to the place where it lay.

If either ball be accidentally moved in complying with this Rule, no penalty shall be incurred, and the ball so moved shall be replaced.

(2) On the putting-green, if a player play when his opponent should have played, the stroke may

be at once recalled by the opponent and the ball replaced.

NOTE.—For a ball which is displaced on a putting-green, see Rule 17 (2) and (3).

For a player playing the opponent's ball on the putting-green, see Rule 20 (1).

For casual water on a putting-green, see Rule 27 (3).

RULE 32

(1) Either side is entitled to have the flag-stick removed when approaching the hole ; if a player's ball strike the flag-stick, which has been so removed by himself, or his partner, or either of their caddies, his side shall lose the hole.

If the ball rest against the flag-stick which is in the hole, the player shall be entitled to remove the flag-stick, and, if the ball fall into the hole, the player shall be deemed to have holed out at his last stroke.

(2) If the player's ball knock the opponent's ball into the hole, the opponent shall be deemed to have holed out at his last stroke.

If the player's ball move the opponent's ball, the opponent, if he choose, may replace it, but this must be done before another stroke is played by either side.

If the player's ball stop on the spot formerly occupied by the opponent's ball, and the opponent declare his intention to replace his ball, the player shall first play another stroke, after which the opponent shall replace and play his ball.

(3) If the player has holed out and the opponent

then plays to the lip of the hole, the player may not knock the ball away, but the opponent, if asked, shall play his next stroke without delay.

If the opponent's ball lie on the lip of the hole, the player, after holing out, may knock the ball away, claiming the hole if holing at the like, and the half if holing at the odd, provided that the player's ball does not strike the opponent's ball and set it in motion ; if the player neglect to knock away the opponent's ball, and it fall into the hole, the opponent shall be deemed to have holed out at his last stroke.

RULE 33

When a player has holed out and his opponent has been left with a stroke for the half, nothing that the player who has holed out can do shall deprive him of the half which he has already gained.

GENERAL PENALTY

RULE 34

Where no penalty for the breach of a Rule is stated, the penalty shall be the loss of the hole.

DISPUTES

RULE 35

An umpire or referee (see Definition 22), when appointed, shall take cognisance of any breach of rule that he may observe, whether he be appealed to on the point or not.

RULE 36

If a dispute arise on any point, a claim must be made before the players strike off from the next teeing-ground, or, in the case of the last hole of the round, before they leave the putting-green. If no umpire or referee has been appointed the players have the right of determining to whom the point shall be referred, but should they not agree, either side may have it referred officially through the Secretary of the Club, to the Rules of Golf Committee, whose decision shall be final. If the point in dispute be not covered by the Rules of Golf, the arbiters shall decide it by equity.

If the players have agreed to an umpire or referee, they must abide by his decision.

SPECIAL RULES FOR MATCH PLAY COMPETITIONS

RULE 1

On the putting-green, if the competitor whose ball is the nearer to the hole play first, his ball shall be at once replaced.

The penalty for a breach of this Rule shall be the disqualification of both competitors.

RULE 2

Competitors shall not agree to exclude the operation of any Rule or Local Rule, nor to waive any penalty incurred in the course of the match, under penalty of their disqualification.

The Rules of Golf Committee recommends that players should not concede putts to their opponents.

RULES FOR THREE-BALL, BEST-BALL AND FOUR-BALL MATCHES

DEFINITIONS

(1) When three players play against each other, each playing his own ball, the match is called a three-ball match.

(2) When one player plays his ball against the best ball of two or more players, the match is called a best-ball match.

(3) When two players play their better ball against the better ball of two other players, the match is called a four-ball match.

GENERAL

RULE 1

Any player may have any ball in the match lifted or played, at the option of its owner, if he consider that it might interfere with or be of assistance to a player or side, but this should only be done before the player has played his stroke.

RULE 2

If a player's ball move any other ball in the match, the moved ball must be replaced as near as possible to the spot where it lay, without penalty.

RULE 3

Through the green a player shall incur no penalty for playing when an opponent should have done so, and the stroke shall not be recalled.

On the putting-green the stroke may be recalled by an opponent, but no penalty shall be incurred.

THREE-BALL MATCHES

RULE 4

During a three-ball match, if no player is entitled at a teeing-ground to claim the honour from both opponents, the same order of striking shall be followed as at the last teeing-ground.

RULE 5

In a three-ball match, if a player's ball strike, or be stopped, or moved by an opponent or an opponent's caddie or clubs, that opponent shall lose the hole to the player. As regards the other opponent the occurrence shall be treated as a rub of the green.

BEST-BALL AND FOUR-BALL MATCHES

RULE 6

Balls belonging to the same side may be played in the order the side deems best.

RULE 7

If a player's ball strike, or be stopped, or moved by an opponent, or an opponent's caddie or clubs, the opponent's side shall lose the hole.

RULE 8

If a player's ball (the player being one of a side) strike, or be stopped by himself, or his partner, or either of their caddies or clubs, only that player shall be disqualified for that hole.

Rule 9

If a player play a stroke with his partner's ball, and the mistake be discovered and intimated to the other side before an opponent has played another stroke, the player shall be disqualified for that hole, and his partner shall drop a ball as near as possible to the spot from which his ball was played, without penalty.   If the mistake be not discovered till after the opponent has played a stroke, the player's side shall lose the hole.

Rule 10

In all other cases where a player would by the Rules of Golf incur the loss of the hole, he shall be disqualified for that hole, but the disqualification shall not apply to his partner.

SPECIAL RULES FOR STROKE COMPETITIONS

Wherever the word Committee is used in these Rules, it refers to the Committee in charge of the Competition.

Rule 1

(1) In Stroke Competitions the competitor who holes the stipulated round or rounds in the fewest strokes shall be the winner.

(2) Competitors shall play in couples; if from any cause there be a single competitor, the Committee shall either provide him with a player who shall mark for him, or select a marker for him and allow him to compete alone.

The order and times of starting should, when possible, be determined by ballot.

RULE 2

(1) Competitors shall start in the order and at the times arranged by the Committee. They shall not discontinue play nor delay to start on account of bad weather or for any other reason whatever, except such as the Committee may consider satisfactory.

The penalty for a breach of this Rule shall be disqualification.

(2) If the Committee consider that the course is not in a playable condition, or that insufficient light renders the proper playing of the game impossible, it shall at any time have power to declare the day's play null and void.

RULE 3

If the lowest scores be made by two or more competitors, the tie or ties shall be decided by another round to be played on the same day ; but if the Committee determine that this is inexpedient or impossible, it shall appoint a day and time for the decision of the tie or ties.

Should an uneven number of competitors tie, their names shall be drawn by ballot and placed upon a list ; the competitors shall then play in couples in the order in which their names appear. The single competitor shall be provided for by the Committee either under Rule 1 (2), or by allowing three competitors to play together if their unanimous consent has been obtained.

RULE 4

(1) New holes should be made on the day on which Stroke Competitions begin.

(2) On the day of the Competition, before starting, no competitor shall play on, or on to, any of the putting-greens, nor shall he intentionally play at any hole of the stipulated round which is within his reach, under penalty of disqualification.

RULE 5

(1) The score for each hole shall be kept by a marker or by each competitor noting the other's score. Should more than one marker keep a score, each shall sign the part of the score for which he is responsible. The scores should be called out after each hole. On completion of the stipulated round the card shall be signed by the person who has marked it, and the competitor shall see that it is handed in as soon as reasonably possible.

The penalty for a breach of this Rule shall be disqualification.

Scoring cards should be issued with the date and the player's name entered on the card.

(2) Competitors must satisfy themselves before the cards are handed in that the scores for each hole are correctly marked, as no alteration can be made on any card after it has been returned. If it be found that a competitor has returned a score lower than that actually played, he shall be disqualified. For the additions of the scores marked the Committee shall be responsible.

(3) If, on the completion of the stipulated round, a player is doubtful whether he has incurred a penalty at any hole, he may enclose his scoring card with a written statement of the circumstances to the

Committee, who shall decide what penalty, if any, has been incurred.

RULES FOR PLAY IN STROKE COMPETITIONS

RULE 6

A competitor shall not ask for nor willingly receive advice from anyone except his caddie.

The penalty for a breach of this Rule shall be disqualification.

RULE 7

(1) Competitors should strike off from the first teeing-ground in the order in which their names appear upon the starting list.

Thereafter the honour shall be taken as in match play, but if a competitor by mistake play out of turn, no penalty shall be incurred, and the stroke cannot be recalled.

(2) If at any hole a competitor play his first stroke from outside the limits of the teeing-ground, he shall count that stroke, tee a ball, and play his second stroke from within these limits.

The penalty for a breach of this Rule shall be disqualification.

RULE 8

(1) A competitor shall hole out with his own ball at every hole.

The penalty for a breach of this Rule shall be disqualification.

(2) If a competitor play a stroke with a ball other than his own, he shall incur no penalty provided

he then play his own ball ; but if he play two consecutive strokes with a wrong ball, he shall be disqualified.

(3) In a hazard, if a competitor play more than one stroke with a ball other than his own and the mistake be discovered before he has played a stroke with the wrong ball from outside the limits of the hazard, he shall incur no penalty provided he then play his own ball.

The penalty for a breach of this Rule shall be disqualification.

RULE 9

If a competitor's ball strike or be stopped by himself, his clubs, or his caddie, the penalty shall be one stroke, except as provided for in Stroke Rule 13 (1).

RULE 10

(1) If a competitor's ball strike or be stopped by another competitor, or his clubs, or his caddie, it is a rub of the green, and the ball shall be played from where it lies, except as provided for in Stroke Rule 13 (1). If a competitor's ball which is at rest be accidentally moved by another competitor, or his caddie, or his clubs, or his ball, or any outside agency except wind, it shall be replaced as near as possible to the spot where it lay.

The penalty for a breach of this Rule shall be disqualification.

(2) A competitor may have any other player's ball played or lifted, at the option of its owner, if he find that it interferes with his play.

RULE 11

A ball may be lifted from any place on the Course. If a player lift a ball under the provisions of this Rule he shall either :

(1) Play a ball as provided for in Rule 22 ; or

(2) Tee and play a ball, under penalty of two strokes, behind the place from which the ball was lifted ; if this be impossible he shall tee and play a ball, under penalty of two strokes as near as possible to the place from which the ball was lifted, but not nearer to the hole.

In preparing a tee as above authorised, the player is exempted from the restrictions imposed by Rule 15.

The penalty for a breach of this Rule shall be disqualification.

RULE 12

For the purpose of identification, a competitor may at any time lift and carefully replace his ball in the presence of the player with whom he is competing.

The penalty for a breach of this Rule shall be one stroke.

RULE 13

(1) When a competitor's ball lying within twenty yards of the hole is played and strikes, or is stopped by, the flag-stick or the person standing at the hole, the penalty shall be two strokes.

(2) When both balls are on the putting-green, if a competitor's ball strike the ball of the player with whom he is competing, the competitor shall incur a

penalty of one stroke, and the ball which was struck shall be at once replaced (see Stroke Rule 10 (1)).

(3) The competitor whose ball is the farther from the hole may have the ball which is nearer to the hole lifted or played at the option of its owner. If the latter refuse to comply with this Rule when requested to do so, he shall be disqualified.

(4) If the competitor whose ball is the nearer to the hole consider that his ball might be of assistance to the player with whom he is competing, he should lift it or play first.

(5) If the competitor whose ball is the nearer to the hole lift his ball while the player's ball is in motion, he shall incur a penalty of one stroke.

(6) If a competitor or his caddie pick up his ball from the putting-green before it is holed out (except as provided for above), he shall, before he has struck off from the next tee, or, in the case of the last hole of the round, before he has left the putting-green, be permitted to replace the ball under penalty of two strokes.

Rule 14

Where in the Rules of Golf the penalty for the breach of any Rule is the loss of the hole, in Stroke Competitions the penalty shall be the loss of two strokes, except where otherwise provided for in these Special Rules.

Rule 15

The Rules of Golf, so far as they are not at variance with these Special Rules, shall apply to Stroke Competitions.

RULE 16

If a dispute arise on any point it shall be decided by the Committee, whose decision shall be final, unless an appeal be made to the Rules of Golf Committee, as provided for in Rule 36.

RULES FOR BOGEY COMPETITIONS

A Bogey Competition is a form of Stroke Competition in which play is against a fixed score at each hole of the stipulated round or rounds.

The reckoning is made as in Match Play, and the winner is the competitor who is most successful in the aggregate of holes. The Rules for Stroke Competitions shall apply with the following exceptions :

(1) Any hole for which a competitor makes no return shall be regarded as a loss. The marker shall only be responsible for the marking of the correct number of strokes at each hole at which a competitor makes a score either equal to or less than the fixed score.

(2) Any breach of Rule which entails the penalty of disqualification shall only disqualify the competitor for the hole at which the breach of Rule occurred ; but a competitor shall not be exempted from the general disqualification imposed by Stroke Rules 2 (1), 4 (2), and 5 (1) and (2).

Note.—A scale showing the handicap allowance, and indicating the holes at which strokes are to be given or taken, shall be printed on the back of every scoring card.

RECOMMENDATIONS FOR LOCAL RULES

When necessary, Local Rules should be made for such obstructions as rushes, trees, hedges, fixed seats, fences, gates, railways, and walls; for such difficulties as rabbit scrapes, hoof marks, and other damage caused to the course by animals; for such local conditions as the existence of mud which may be held to interfere with the proper playing of the game, and for the penalty to be imposed in the case of a ball which lies out of bounds, see Rule 23 (1).

When a ball is lifted under a Local Rule, as in the case of a ball lifted from a putting-green other than that of the hole which is being played, the Rules of Golf Committee recommends that if it is to be played from " through the green," it should be *dropped ;* if it is to be played on the putting-green of the hole that is being played, it should be *placed.*

FORM AND MAKE OF GOLF CLUBS AND BALLS

The Rules of Golf Committee intimates that it will not sanction any substantial departure from the traditional and accepted form and make of Golf Clubs, which, in its opinion, consist of a plain shaft and a head which does not contain any mechanical contrivance, such as springs; it also regards as illegal the use of such clubs as those of the mallet-headed type, or such clubs as have the neck so bent as to produce a similar effect.

Note.—The Rules of Golf Committee intimates

that the following general considerations will guide
it in interpreting this Rule :—

(1) The head of a Golf Club shall be so constructed
that the length of the head from the back of the heel
to the toe shall be greater than the breadth from the
face to the back of the head.

(2) The shaft shall be fixed to the heel, or to a
neck, socket, or hose which terminates at the heel.

(3) The lower part of the shaft shall, if produced,
meet the heel of the club, or (as for example in the
case of the Park and Fairlie Clubs) a point opposite
the heel, either to right or left, when the club is soled
in the ordinary position for play.

The weight of the ball shall be not greater than
1·62 ounces avoirdupois, and the size not less than
1·62 inches in diameter. The Rules of Golf Committee will take whatever steps it thinks necessary
to limit the power of the ball with regard to distance,
should any ball of greater power be introduced.

ETIQUETTE OF GOLF

(1) No one should stand close to or directly
behind the ball, move, or talk, when a player is
making a stroke.

On the putting-green no one should stand beyond
the hole in the line of a player's stroke.

(2) The player who has the honour should be
allowed to play before his opponent tees his ball.

(3) No player should play from the tee until the
party in front have played their second strokes and
are out of range, nor play up to the putting-green

till the party in front have holed out and moved
away.

(4) Players who have holed out should not try
their putts over again when other players are
following them.

(5) Players looking for a lost ball should allow
other matches coming up to pass them ; they
should signal to the players following them to pass,
and having given such a signal, they should not continue their play until these players have passed and
are out of reach.

(6) Turf cut or displaced by a player should be
at once replaced and pressed down with the foot.

(7) A player should carefully fill up all holes made
by himself in a bunker.

(8) Players should see that their caddies do not
injure the holes by standing close to them when the
ground is soft.

(9) A player who has incurred a penalty stroke
should intimate the fact to his opponent as soon as
possible.

GOLFING TERMS

Bisques.—Strokes conceded by one side to another
in Match play, but differing from the strokes
ordinarily given in that the receiver may use them
as he pleases.   He may take the strokes allowed to
him singly or together at any hole or holes.   The
side receiving bisques does not require to declare
that a stroke or strokes is being taken until the hole
is played out.

Bogey.—The number of strokes that should be

taken to each hole by a scratch player after making allowance for difficulties in the course. Thus, a very difficult four-stroke hole under Par might be a Bogey five. The Bogey for each hole is fixed locally and printed on the club card.

Dormie.—A side is " dormie " when it is as many holes up as there are holes remaining to be played.

Eclectic Competitions.—A stroke competition in which each competitor plays two rounds of eighteen holes and counts the best score which has been made at each hole in the two rounds. The total for eighteen holes thus obtained forms the Eclectic score.

Par Play.—Perfect golf without flukes is called Par play. Thus, if a green can be reached in two strokes, the hole is a Par four, two putts being allowed on each green.

Stymie.—A player is stymied if, on the putting-green, his opponent's ball lies in the line of his putt to the hole, provided the balls be not within six inches of each other.